COMPUTER SKILLS
Acquisition

(Second Edition)

Emmanuel Olomu

Computer Skills Acquisition

Copyright (c) 2023 Second Edition

African Forensic Academy,
Ogun State
oladiipoolomu@gmail.com
Tel: 07066280094

PREFACE

The purpose of this book is to help people from different fields of life, the students, busy Executives, Secretaries, Lawyers, Engineers, Medical Personnel, Computer Operators, Ministers of God, to acquire computer skill that can help them in their various jobs. This book will not only be useful for the beginners but also for computer literate who want to know more about computer usage.

New topics like digital marketing, the use of artificial Intelligence in business, computer hazards and side effect of internet on the youth are introduced to make some dim issues in computer profession clearer.

To get the best out of this book. It is recommended that this book be studied according to the order in which it is presented, that is, module one first, followed by module two up to the last module. At the end of each module review question are provided.

Olomu Emmanuel Oladiipo *FFIS* '

MODULE ONE

In this module you will learn the following:
- Definition of computer
- Classification of Computer
- Types of computers
- Hardware; input and output devices
Features of windows How to use windows

CHAPTER ONE

1.0   Introduction To Computer System

1.1   What is A Computer?

A computer is an electronic device that works by following a set of coded instructions. A computer performs four major tasks

> a. accepts data
> b. processes data
> c. produces output
> d. stores results

A computer, can therefore be defined as an electronic device that is capable of accepting data automatically, process it and produce the desired result that can be stored for future use.

1.2   Classification of computer

a.   Digital Computer: This counts, i.e it operates directly on a discrete quantity of numbers and presentations, and present the data to the machine in binary digits *(Os and 1s).   e.g.* calculators, adding machines, mobile phones and personal computers.

b.   Analog: This   measures, i.e.,   it   represents information by measuring the change in physical quantities like temperature, e.g thermometer, Anemometer, oscilloscope, television, autopilot, speedometer, etc

c.   Hybrid Computer: This has the capacity of both an Analog and a Digital computer; it is used for weather observation, research, production industries, and space exploration. It is also called digit-analogue computer.   Examples are Gasoline   Station, Electrocardiogram Machine etc.

1.3 Type of Computer.

i.   Micro Computer: These are computers designed for homes, businesses and offices usually referred to as personal computer (pc).
The most compact are called laptops and palmtops. These set of computers use microprocessors in their central processing unit; hence they are called microcomputers.

ii.   Mini Computer: This is a mid-level computer built to perform complex computations while dealing efficiently with a high Level of input and output from users connected via terminals. Mini computers also frequently connected to other minicomputers on a network and distribute processing among all the attached machines. Minicomputers are used heavily in transaction-processing applications and as interfaces between mainframe computer systems and wide area networks,

iii.   Mainframe Computer: This is the largest computer designed for the very intensive computational jobs, it can be shared by multiple users connected to the computer via terminals. Supercomputers, which are the most powerful mainframes, perform highly complex and time-consuming computations. Mainframes are used in research by scientists, large banks, and the military.

This book is basically on micro-computer, so most

of our discussions will be on it as the knowledge of micro-computer is applicable to the other types of computers. Moreover, because of the advancement in technology new micro-computers are now performing the job that was formerly exclusively reserved for mini or mainframe.

1.4   Hardware

The Hardware are the components of the computer that can be seen or touched. It can be divided into the following:

a.   Central Processing Unit (CPU);
The CPU is made up of the Arithmetic and Logic Unit, the Control unit and the Memory.

b.   The peripheral devices; any device attached to the CPU like the monitor, printer, scanner, mouse, keyboard etc. is known as peripheral devices.

Hardware can be categorized into input and output devices.

1.5   Input Devices

These devices enable a computer user to enter data, commands, and programs into the CPU. The most common input device is the keyboard. Data typed at the typewriter-like keyboard is translated by the computer into recognisable patterns.

1.6   The Keyboard

The keyboard can be divided into four parts namely;

i.   **Numeric key pad:** This is at the foremost right part of the keyboard and it is designed for quick input of numbers most of the keys carry double functions.

ii.   **The alphanumeric keys:** This helps in making

input with letters and numbers, punctuation and special characters.

iii. **Special Keys:** (ctrl, shift, Tab, Alt, Enter etc) These are used for different functions such as to delete or enter data or issue command, print screen, esc, etc most of the keys work in combination with other keys, for example Ctrl + P will reboot the system etc.

Back Space key: This key deletes towards the left side of the cursor.
Delete Key: This deletes to the right side of the cursor **Enter Key:** This key is used to force down the cursor to the next line.
Shift Key: When this key is press down it bring out the second function of the keys that carry double functions e.g shift+7 = &, shift =).
Tab Key: This is used to push the text or create a space to the right, (0.5 or an inch at a time) **pg dn, pg up:** This moves the cursor up or down the page at a time.
Arrow Keys: These are used to move the cursor in the direction of the arrows.
Home Key: Moves the cursor to the beginning of a line.
End Key: Moves the cursor to the end of a line.

iv. Function Keys: *(F1, F2,F3,* F4,...F12)These performs different function in different packages,; some are used alone, while others in combination with other special keys e.g Alt+F4 closes the current package, F1 is for help etc.

There are packages writing purposely for training users on how to use keyboard. I recommend you install any of these packages on your computer to train you on keyboard usage. Examples of these packages are Mavis Beacon, Typing Tutor or Mario Teaches Typing.

A Keyboard-fig 1.0

1.7 Other Input Devices

Other input devices include the mouse, which translates physical motion into motion on a computer video display screen; the joystick, which performs the same function, and is favoured for computer games; the trackball, on laptops; scanners which "read" words or symbols on a printed page and translates them into electronic patterns that the computer can manipulate and store; light pens, which can be used to "write" directly on the monitor screen; voice recognition systems, which take spoken words and translate them into digital signals for the computer and web cam used in capturing motion pictures into the system.

Mouse - fig 1.1

A Mouse is a hand-held device that controls the movement of a pointer on your screen. There are many mice in the market but the best mouse is the one that is designed to comfort your fingers and wrist.

Webcam fig 1.2

Microphone fig 1.3

1.8 Output Devices

These devices enable the user to see or have the results of the computer's calculations or data manipulations. For example, through the monitor the user sees the image (soft copy) of the work been done in the CPU. Also, the Printer enables the user to have the printed job (hard copy) and through the speaker the sound can be clearly heard.

Computer monitor- fig *1.4*

Printer fig *1.5*

Speaker *fig 1.6*

1.9   Storage Devices

Computer systems can store data internally {in memory) and externally (on storage devices). Internally, instructions or data can be temporarily stored in silicon RAM (Random Access Memory) chips that are mounted directly on the computer's main circuit board, or in chips mounted on peripheral cards plugged into the computer's main circuit board.

Hard, or "fixed", disks cannot be removed from their disk-drive cabinets, which contain the electronics to read and write data on to the magnetic disk surfaces. Hard disks currently used with personal computers can store several gigabytes of information. CDROM, DVD-ROM technology, normally produces storage capacities up to about 700 megabytes and 4 gigabytes respectively.

1.10   I/O Device (input/output)

There are devices that serve both as input devices and output devices e.g., Compact Disks, memory card, and flash drive can be used to input in data into the system or output data from it. Hence, they are called I/O Devices.

Flash Drive fig 1.7   Compact Disk (CD) -fig 1.8

1.11 Drive
A drive is a device use to read or write data from or unto the storage medium. The following devices use the corresponding drive:
Compact Disk(CD) uses CD-ROM/CD Writer Drive, DVD (Digital Video Disk) uses DVD-ROM/Writer Drive"

NOTE: Flash drive has its own drive embedded on its chip so it is plugged into the computer board using any available USB Port.

Hard disk also has its drive embedded on its chip, so, it can be attached to the modern board in its place or connected via USB port if it is an external hard disk.

1.12 Cursor Movement

Cursor is the blinking character on the screen that shows the insertion point of whatever you type from the keyboard You move your cursor around documents using either the mouse or the keyboard. You can click on the horizontal scroll bar or click and drag the tab on the horizontal bar to move up or down. (Try this and see how it works).

Note: If you are asked to double-click an item: Point to the item with your arrow by moving the mouse. Quickly press your left mouse

If you are asked to right-click: Point to the item with your arrow by moving the mouse. Press your right mouse button.

1.13   Units of Measurement of Information. Computer information is measured in bits; this is the smallest unit of information storable in a computer or peripheral device, expressed as 0 or 1. Eight bits make a byte, the common measure of memory or storage capacity.

Eight (8) bits make one (1) byte, 1,024 bytes equals 1 kilobytes, 1,048,576 bytes equals 1' megabyte (ie. One million bytes), 1 billion bytes equals one gigabyte. Take not that computer does not use base ten(decimal) system like human but base two i.e binary system.

Computer storage and memory is often measured in megabytes (MB) and gigabytes (GB). A small book contains about 1 MB of information. 1 MB is 1,024 kilobytes, or 1,048,576 (1024x1024) bytes, not one million bytes.

Similarly, one 1 GB is 1,024 MB, or 1,073,741,824 (1024x1024x1024) bytes. A terabyte (TB) is 1,024 GB; 1 TB is about the same amount of information as all of the books in a large library, or roughly 1,610 CDs worth of data. A petabyte (PB) is 1,024 TB. 1 PB of data, if written on DVDs, would create roughly 223,100 DVDs, i.e., a stack about 878 feet tall, or a stack of CDs a mile high. Indiana University is now building storage systems capable of holding petabytes of data. An exabyte (EB) is 1,024 PB. A zettabyte (ZB) is 1,024 EB. Finally, a yottabyte (YB) is 1,024 ZB.

Unit	Equivalent
1 kilobyte (KB)	1,024 bytes
1 megabyte (MB)	1,048,576 bytes
1 gigabyte (GB)	1,073,741,824 bytes
1 terabyte (TB)	1,099,511,627,776 bytes
1 petabyte (PB)	1,125,899,906,842,624 bytes

Review Question

1. Define computer.
2. Discuss on the classes and types of computers we have.
3. Mention three storage devices and their corresponding drives.
4. Why is flash drive considered to be external storage media?
5. Computer performs four major tasks. Mention them.
6. Explain what you understand by units of measurement of information.

CHAPTER TWO

2.0   SOFTWARE

2.1   Introduction to Software.

A software is a set of coded instructions that computer follows in order to accomplish a task.

Software can be basically categorised into:
  a. System Software.
  b. Application Software.

2.2   The system software

This controls the workings of the computer including some basic routine functions. It consists of Operating system (OS), the translators, a computer program that converts other programs from one computer language into another and the utilities use in carrying out basic maintenance work on the system e.g disk defragmenter. Examples of operating systems are Windows, Unix, DOS, etc.

2.3 Operating System

An Operating system is the master of programs that controls and manages the resources of computers, without it the system will not work. Basically, an operating system controls movement of data to and fro the keyboard, screen or monitor, disk and other peripheral devices. It provides users with all the necessary commands needed to communicate with the computer system.

Functions of Operating System

1. It controls the way the computer uses stored programs in the memory or auxiliary storage such as floppy diskettes(floppy diskette is no more in use), flash drive, CD-ROM or DVD-ROM. External hard disk)

2. ft serves as basement for application software

3. It interprets whatever information is keyed in from the keyboard or input devices into the computer.

4. It simplifies the creation and management of files.

5. It handles error recovery and condition

2.4   Types of Operating System

i. Single-User operating system

This is an operating system that makes the computer machine independently available to only one user at a time. They are called DISK OPERATING SYSTEM (DOS) Examples are MS-DOS, IBM-DOS etc.

ii. Multi-user Operating System

It is the operating system that allows more than two users to work with the computer at the same time. Examples are UNIX, XENIX, PSMOS, WINDOWS etc. However, for the purpose of this book we shall be treating Windows.

2.5   **Application software**

This addresses the multitude of tasks for which people use computers. Application software performs jobs such as word processing, database management, desktop publishing packages and the like. Some are written on demand to meet some specific needs of the user, *(i. e they are customised software)* like the Medical Reports software for a diagnostic and clinical organisation, Software to take inventory of a company, the one written for the purpose of entering data of a school students etc. Application software are also known as application packages. For more information on application packages go to *module two, chapter five.*

2.6   **Booting**

This is the process of starting or resetting a computer.

A boot can be "cold", as when the machine is first turned on, or "warm", which typically means reloading just the computer's operating system without the POST process.

2.7   Cold Booting

Cold booting is the switching on of the computer i.e. Starting up the computer with the use of power switch. Immediately the computer is on it will put on a self-test called POST i.e. Put On Self-Test. To check the correct connection of the computer parts such as the hard disk, keyboard, monitor, memory etc. If any of these parts are not well connected it will indicate by an error message on the screen (monitor) or by making unusual beeping

sound.   A Desktop Computer -

fig.2.0

A Laptop Computer *fig2.1*

2.8   Desktop:
Steps to be taken in Cold Booting

1.   Make sure the connections are properly done.
2.   Switch on the power supply from main switch
3.   Put on the UPS (uninterruptible power supply).
4.   Press the power button on the System Unit (you will see a light indicating the System Unit is ready to operate)
5.   Press the power button on the Monitor. It will display a light, indicating that it is ready for operation.

2.9   Laptop:
Steps to be taken in Cold Booting

1. Connect the charger to the power supply
2. Open up the computer, and adjust the monitor to be at the right angle.

Review Questions

1. What is warm booting?
2. How do you connect and boot Laptop computer?
3. What is an Operating System?
4. Mention five functions of an Operating System.
5. Define software.
6. What is an application software?
7. Explain the difference and 'similarity between a keyboard and a mouse
8. Mention all the keys on computer keyboard and their functions.

CHAPTER THREE

3.0 WINDOWS
AND ITS ENVIRONMENT

3.1 Introduction
Windows is an operating system developed by Microsoft hence its called Microsoft windows. It is an interface between the user and the computer system. It gives the user the access to other programmes on the system. It is easy to operate because of the use of graphic user interface (GUI), all a user needs to do is to click on icons that help to command the computer to perform certain function. There are versions, each new version has greater capabilities than the older one examples are windows 2000, XP, 10 etc.

3.2   Features of Windows

3.3   The Desktop

Fig 3.0

Desktop is the first background a user sees after the booting process. Each icon on the desktop represents a programme such as a package, folder or computer utility, depending on the setup of a system, the arrangement of the Icons may be different from one computer to the other.

3.4 Taskbar and Start Button

The taskbar is usually situated at the bottom of the desktop screen and the start button is usually at the bottom right conner of the desktop screen. The taskbar and start button are used to navigate through windows. Both features are always available on your desktop, no matter how many windows you have opened.

The buttons on the taskbar show you which windows of programs are open, even if some windows are minimized or hidden beneath another window. You can easily switch to a different window by clicking its taskbar button.

Fig 3.1 Taskbar

Fig 3.2 Start Button

Fig 3.3 Start menu

3.5   How to Use the Start Menu.

1.   Click the start button.
      The start menu appears.
2.   Click the item you want to open.

3.6   This PC *(called My Computer In the older windows)*

This PC

fig 3.4

This PC can be used to view the contents of a drive, folder or network. When you double-click This PC on your desktop, available drives appear in a new window. When you double-click a drive icon (e.g hard disk, flash drive and CD), a window display the folders and files contained in that drive. When you double-click on a folder it opens up the files it contains.

3.7 To Start a Program.

1. Click the start button, and then search for the program and click.

OR.

2. Go to desktop search for the Icon if it is there double click on the program Icon

OR

3. Go to the task bar, if the program's icon is there double click on it to open

3.8 To Quit a Program.

Click the closed button in the upper-right corner of the program's window.

3.9 Creating Folders

fig 3.4

When you use a program and save your work, or when you install a program, you're creating files. You can store your files in many locationson the hard disk, a network drive, flash drive, and so on. To organize your files better, you can also store them in folders.

3.10 How to Create Folders

1. On the desktop, double-click on This PC.

"This PC" window appears.

2.   Double-click the disk drive or folder in which you want to create folder. The drive or folder appears.

3.   On the file menu, point to New and then click Folder.

4.   Type a folder name, and then press ENTER.

The new folder appears in the location you selected.

When you are giving names to files in Windows, the file name can be up to 255 characters, including spaces. But file names cannot contain any of the following characters: *\ / < > " |.

3.11   Find /Search Command

When you're looking for a particular folder or file, you can use Search or Find command. You can use the Search/Find command on the Start menu to quickly search your entire computer-or a specific folder or drive.

To find a file or folder
1. Click the Start button, click on Search box
2. Type the name of file or folder you want to find.
3.   Specify where to search.
4.   Click search or press Enter.

After a moment, the result of the search appears.

3.12 Opening Files and Folders.

After you've located the file you want, you can double-click to open it.

3.13 To Open File Or Folder

1.   On the desktop, double-click This PC. The This PC window appears,

2.   Double-click the drive that contains the file or folder you want to open.

3.   Double-click the file or folder.

3.14   Renaming Files and Folders.

If you decide to change the name of a file or folder, you can quickly rename it.

3.15   To Rename a File or Folder.

1.   In a window, select the file or folder you want to rename..

2.   On the file menu, click Rename.

3.   Type a name, and then press ENTER.

3.16 To Copy or Move a File or Folder.

1.   select the file or folder you want to copy or move.

2.   click Copy to copy the file (CTRL+C), or click Cut (CTRL+X) to move the file.

3.   Double-click the folder in which you want to place the file or folder

4.   Paste (CTRL+V) or (SHIFT+INSERT). The file appears in its new location.

3.17 Working with Frequently Used Files and Folders

The start menu lists the document used most recently, so that you can quickly reopen them.

A shortcut can be created to access the frequently used files. A shortcut doesn't change the location of a file- the shortcut is just a pointer that lets you open the file quickly. If you delete the shortcut, the original file isn't deleted.

3.18. o Open Recently Used Document.

1.   Click the start button, and
     then point t
     A list of your recently opened document
2.   Click a document on the list.
     The document opens.

3.19   To move a file to the My Documents folder.
Drag the file to the My Documents folder on your desktop and release it.

3.20   To create a shortcut to a file.

1. Use the right mouse button to drag the file to the desktop.
2.   On the menu that appears, click Create shortcut(s) here.

The shortcut appears on the desktop. You can COPY or move the shortcut to another location.

3.21   Recycle Bin

Recycle Bin is the place where all files deleted on the computer are temporarily stored. If you change your mind, you can restore the file. But, when the Recycle Bin is emptied, all of the items in it are permanently deleted from your computer. Go to the desktop and locate an icon named Recycle Bin.

3.22   To Delete Files and Folders.

1. On the desktop, double-click This PC. The This PC window appears.
2.   Select the file and folder you want to delete.
3. On the File menu, click Delete.
The Confirm File Delete dialog box appears.
4. Click Yes.

The file is moved to the Recycle Bin.

3.23 To Permanently Delete Files and Folders.

1. On the desktop, double-click Recycle Bin. The Recycle Bin opens.
2. On the File menu, click Empty Recycle Bin.

3.24   Shutting Down Command

The Shut Down command on the start menu close windows and programs and prepare your computer for shutting down. If you haven't already saved your work, you're prompted to do so. If you turn off your computer without shutting it down correctly, you may lose your data.

3.25   To shut down your computer.

1. Click the Start button and go to the list of options given. The options are; Switch User, Log Off, Lock, Restart, Sleep, Hibernate, Shut Down.

2. Chose Shut Down.
The shortcut for shutting down is Alt+F4

Review Questions
1. What do you understand by Windows?
2. Mention five features of Windows and their functions.
3. How do you use My Computer to list the content of drive E?
4. How do you search for a file named Tiwa on drive C?
5. Create a folder named mycv under Document.

CHAPTER FOUR

4.0   Computer Security And Hazard *(User Safety)*

4.1   What is Computer Security?

Computer security is the method put in place to prevent standalone and networked computer systems from being damaged by people either consciously or unconsciously, like the unauthorised use of applications, breaking into organisations' databases, stealing of data/information, and deliberate software and hardware sabotage.

As far as a computer system is connected to the internet, system intruders called hackers or crackers can break into your system from anywhere in the world if proper measure *is* not put in place.

Some hackers break into peoples' system purposely to prove their technological worth *(at times an organization may implore the service of an Hacker to know how secure its data base is), this type of hacker are being refer to as ethical hackers,* while crackers break into peoples' database purposely for malicious intentions such as fraud after stealing ones password, credit card numbers, data on the hard disk etc., this can lead to loss of huge amount of money and can cause a setback for any organization or an individual.

Today, the word hacker is used to denote internet "rubber", anyone who steals money or data, by breaking into another man's online account or lure his victim into releasing login detail or personal information.

4.2. Malicious Software *(Malware)*

Malicious software also known as Malware are programs/software written by obsessed programmers for malicious intentions. Examples of these programs are computer virus, spyware, worms, ransomware.

4.3 Computer Virus

This is a computer program that is part of another legal program and inserts copies of itself, often damaging the integrity of stored data. It travels with the legal program that contains it.

It is a program which disguise itself as something useful, but when run does damage to the computer system such as deleting your data, locking up your hard disk, making your operating system not bootable, filling your hard disk-with its own useless files, etc. while appearing to do something else. Some viruses are so dangerous that they can cause loss of millions of dollars, wasting of time and energy.

4.4. Spyware

A Spyware is a malicious software you install on your computer inadvertently or is install on your computer without your consent by an intruder. The purpose of spyware is to steal your data or spy on one's online activities hence the name spyware.

The increase in transactions over the Internet has greatly increased the chance of attacking networked systems from anywhere in the world.

4.5 Security Measures Against Computer Attack:

a.   Make sure you install recent version of Antiviral program on your system.

b.   Update your antivirus program constantly.

c.   Install and activate firewall program on

your system. (*If one does not accompany your computer from the Manufacturer*)

d.   Do not use a storage media from another computer especially computer connected with the internet without scanning it.

e.   If you are connected to the internet, do not download a program you are not sure of its source.

f.   Install antispyware program on your system if your system does not have Window Defender (*window defender is a program that protects computer from spyware and other malicious programs*).

g.   Do not open an e-mail with attachment from unsolicited source

h.   Unauthorized persons must not be allowed into the   computer room.

i.   Backup all the data on the system using reliable   media

j.   Confidential information must be encrypted.

k.   Use passwords that cannot be easily guessed.

4.6.   Symptoms of Infected Systems

1.   Computer restart without any reasonable cause.

2.   Strange files in the hard disk.

3.   Hard disk becomes inaccessible.

4.   Strange software running on the system.

5.   Keyboard not responding appropriately without a reasonable cause.

6.   System running too slowly without a reasonable cause.

7.   Missing files on the system.

8.   Windows locked up by itself asking you to see administrator.

9.   Documents sent to printer are deleted

before printing.

10. Strange cursor movement without any reasonable reasoning.

4.7. Some Antivirus/Antispyware Programs

i. Avast
ii. MacAfee Antivirus Internet Security
iii. Norton Antivirus and Internet Security
iv. Panda Antivirus
v. Eset Antivirus.

NOTE: Antivirus program must be installed before the virus infection or else it may not be effective or work at all.

4.8 Computer Hazard

There are lot of health hazard caused by the use of computer; Computer Vision Syndrome which is the name given to eye problems caused by prolonged computer use including: Eye irritation and blurred vision also headache and neck pain. The power carries by the CPU cable if there is improper connection can cause a fire outbreak.

4.9 Computer Repetitive Stress Injury (CRSI).

This is the injury caused by excessive and repetitive use of the upper extremities (i .e the fingers, palm and the wrist) and waist. This usually happens when tasks are performed under uncomfortable conditions, using uncomfortable postures and poorly designed equipment. Common tasks that cause CRSI include typing for hours on a computer keyboard, clicking the mouse continuously over a long period of time for days. Treatment includes rest, anti-inflammatory medications and more importantly see your doctor.

4.10 Prevention of Computer Hazard

a. Use the right posture while working e.g an adjustable chair should be used with feet planted firmly on ground while the arms are free to move without obstruction.

b. Avoid stress at work.

c. Take rest between long periods of work like standing up and move around.

d. Use anti glare glasses while working on computer; anti-glare lenses are coated to minimise glare and reflection

e. Use all the electrical part according to the instruction of the manufacturer.

F. Make sure you connect your system properly before using.

g. Off your Lazerjet printers when not in use to reduce radiation emission,

h. Use mouse that is design to comfort your wrist and fingers.

Review Questions

1. Why is the security of the computer important to the user?

2. What do you understand by a computer virus?

3. What are the measures to be taken against computer intruders?

4. Explain what you understand by computer repetitive stress injury.

5.   Mention five (5) ways of preventing computer hazard.

MODULE TWO

In this module you will learn the following:

- Definition of Application Packages
- Types of Application Packages and their uses
- Mode of Acquisition of Packages
- Benefits of Packages to the society.

CHAPTER FIVE

5.0.   **Application Packages**

5.1. What is An Application Package?

An application package is a program or group of programs/software designed for end users. This addresses the multitude of tasks for which people use computers. Applications software cannot run without the operating system and system utilities.

5.2 Types of Packages and Their Uses.

Types of Packages	Uses	Examples
Word Processing package	For creation of documents, typesetting for official and personal use.	Microsoft Word, Microsoft Works, WordPerfect, Notepad, Word Pad, etc.
Database Management Package	For creating database, managing and manipulation of data to get the Desired	MySQL, SQL Server, MongoDB, Oracle Database, PostgreSQL, Informix, Sybase

	information.	
Educational packages	For learning and Productivity, Assessment and Content Reporting, Course Creation. Education and Training Campus Management Tool	Canvas Blackboard Learn Google Classroom Wisenet Workday Student
Desktop Publishing package	For creating documents for publication, eg. Handbills, posters, Textbooks etc.	PageMaker, Publishers, etc.
Web design package	For creation of websites in the internet.	Adobe Dreamweaver. Mobirise. Squarespace. WordPress etc
Graphics package	For creating of graphic document.	CorelDraw, Paint brush, Instant artist etc
email Packages	For Communication, marketing	Yahoo mail, google mail, 0-mail etc.
Media packages	Entertainment, Preaching, Advertisement. Training	Media Player, Cyber link, Power DVD, Power Director.
Social media Packages	Connecting with friends, advertisement etc	Twitter, Facebook, WhatsApp, Instagram,

Video Meetings Packages	Conferences, workshops, seminars, teachings and Meetings	Google meet, Zoom, Microsoft Teams, BlueJeans Meetings, Skype etc

Table 5.0

5.3.   Mode of Acquisitions of Application Packages.

i.   **In-House**:   It can be written by the joint effort of the organization's programmer/ software developer, software analyst and the System Administrator.

ii.   **Leasing**: It can be leased from a software company. This is the best option where the organization has no capable hands that can develop the software and the price of buying a new one is out of reach.

iii.   **Purchasing**: The organization can buy a ready-made package from a software company as far as the package is capable of meeting their demand.

5.4.   Criteria for Package Acceptability:

Before a package can be said to be acceptable the following conditions must be considered:

i.   User friendly: User must be able to use it without any   difficulty.
ii. Documentation: It must be properly documented.
iii. Cost: It must not be too expensive.
iv. The user's Need: It must be able to meet the need of the   user.
v.   Hardware requirement: The user should find

out if the existing hardware is compatible with the package or to get a new hardware, for example, many new packages like CorelDraw 18, Encarta Encyclopedia 2010 will not work with Pentium I, II.
vi. Timing of Process: How long will it takes the package to produce the output.

5.5. The Benefits of Packages to The Society.

The advents of the computer packages and their proliferations have made it possible for computer to be used in different fields. The benefits of computers to society are many, some of them are listed below:

a. Communication

People all over the world are able to communicate, engage and interact with each other using IM, email, blogs, online forums, Voice over internet protocol (VoIP) social media and other options.

b. Work

Computers packages are now used in every sphere of influence, field and sector and across industries. They are used for a variety of tasks, applications and activities and to enhance productivity on all fronts.

c. Education

Computers packages have simplified and streamlined the process of education for millions of people, both undergraduate and postgraduates. Computer package has made it possible for busy people to receive education in the comfort of their houses.

d. Jobs Influence

The widespread use and application of computer packages has created multiple industries, derived sectors and professions and facilitated job opportunities for millions of people.

e. Entertainment

Computer packages on laptops and desktops have turned the personal computers (pc) to all-in-one entertainment systems for millions of users as they watch movies, sports events and news, programs, socialise, download videos and play games.

Review Questions
1. What is an application Package?
2. What are the benefits of computer packages to the Society?
3. Mention (5) types of packages and their uses.
4. What are the criteria for package acceptability?
5. What are the uses of media and communication packages to the entertainment industries?

MODULE THREE

In this module you will learn the following:

- How to start Microsoft Word
- Getting familiar with Microsoft Word
- How to create a new document
- How to create table
- How to format document
- Page Layout
- How to password document
- Word Art
- Printing in Microsoft Word

CHAPTER SIX

6.0   **Microsoft WORD**

6.1.   Introduction To Microsoft Word

Microsoft word is an application Package or software used for word processing activities. One can create, edit, and print a document with Microsoft Word (MS-Word). Some of its versions are Ms-word 2010, Ms-word 2013, Ms-word 2015, Ms-Word 2019 etc. there are always some similarities between the old and the new versions, but the new versions are more sophisticated than the old versions.

In spite of the similarities between the versions of Microsoft word, even an expert in the former versions will still learn one or two things in the new version before he or she can adequately use it.

6.2 Starting Microsoft Word.

A. i.   Click the start button
   ii. search for Word and click

b. An existing document can be opened by going to > taskbar > Documents> click on the filename

C. OR Double click the Word Icon on the Desktop.

6.3. Getting Familiar with Microsoft Word Window

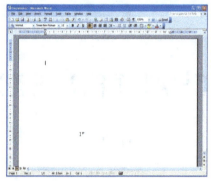

Fig 6.0

6.5. The Quick Access Toolbar

fig 6.1

The Quick Access toolbar provides Access to commands frequently used. By default Save, Undo, and Redo appear on the Quick Access toolbar. Save is used to save file, Undo to rollback an action taken, and Redo to reapply an action rolled back.

6.6. The Ribbon

Commands are clicked to tell Microsoft Word what to

do the Ribbon is used to issue commands. The Ribbon is located near the top of the screen, below the Quick Access toolbar. At the top of the Ribbon are several tabs; clicking a tab displays several related command groups. Within each group are related command buttons. Buttons are clicked to issue commands or to access menus and dialog boxes. Dialog box launcher may also be found in the bottomright corner of a group. Clicking the dialog box launcher gives access to additional commands through a dialog box.

6.7.   How to Create a New Document.

Immediately the Ms-Word Icon is clicked a new page is brought out for you to be used for your typesetting. The default page size is letter but you can change it to A4 size or any size of your choice. MS-Word gives the new document a temporary name until you save it with a supplied name of your choice. You can create a new document quickly by clicking on the blank page button under File Menu OR Press CTRL +N

6.8.   How to Open An Existing Document.

To Open Document You Have Worked On Recently.
MS-Word keeps track of the documents you have worked on recently! You can quickly open one of these documents by the following steps.

1.   Click the File Menu
2.   Search for the document's name and click on it NOTE: the last ten recent files will be listed.

OR

1.   Click on document folder on the taskbar
2.   search for the document and click

6.9. How to Save a Document.

1. Click the on the file menu

2. Click Save As

3. In the Save As dialog box, select the drive or folder where you want to save the document.

4. Choose file format from the option given.

5. Type in the file name in the file name boxes

6. Click save button.

OR Click the Save Button on the Quick Access Toolbar

Hot Keys = CTRL+ S

When you want to save a file for the second time or in subsequent saving of the same document, click save button on the Quick Access Tool bar instead of Save As.

6.10 How to Password Your Documents.

1. Go to file menu and click "Save As" 2. In the file name box, give the document a name

3. Go to Tools.

4. From Tools choose the General option button.

5. Type the Password name in the password to open box, to allow only users who know the password to open the documentation

6. Click Ok button

7. When MS-Word prompts you to confirm the password, retype it

8. Choose Ok button again.

9. Click Save button

10. Close the document

11. Open the document you have just protected with the password

12. What did you notice?

13. Type in a wrong password

14. So what happened? And what was the message the computer displayed?

15. Now type in the correct password

A password can contain up to 15 characters and can include letters symbols and spaces. As you type the password e.g Titilayo, asterisks (*) or bullets (.) are displayed for each character you type. Passwords are case sensitive.

NOTE: for safety or your document keep the records of your password under lock and key and do not choose a password that can be easily guessed by an intruder.

6.11   Closing a Document and Quitting

When you finish working with a document, close it to free the used memory of the computer system.

6.12   To Close A Document

1. Go to file menu

2. Click close

NOTE: if a document has changed (i.e you have added or removed from it) and you have not saved it, MS-Word will ask if you want to save the changes before closing.

If you choose the YES Button but if you have not named the document, MS-Word will display the Save As dialogue box.

6.13. To Quit from Microsoft Word

1. Click File on menu
2. Click Exit or click the Close Button (X) on your title bar on the application window
3. HotKeysALT+F4

6.14   Guideline for Naming Documents.

MS-Word documents can have any valid Ms-Dos file name, using the following rules

i. File names can be from one to eight character long, followed by a period and an optional filename extension of one to three characters. If you do not add a filename extension, MS-Word adds DOC by default.

ii. You can use any characters except the following characters: * ?[ ] + =\/ : <>

6.15   Make it A Habit Protect Your Documents.

A good rule is to save your document constantly, let your hand be on the save button every time. You can use the Automatic save feature to save documents periodically as you work. If you are saving frequently, you will not lose much work if there is a power failure, the application stops running and other problems. It is also a good idea to save a document before you print it or before making major changes to the document.

However, if you actually save your document on the hard-disk, you should also have backup of important documents on other drives like the flash drive, Compact

Disk, google drive etc.

6.16   **Formatting Text**:

Formatting enables you to change the front type, size or bold, subscript, text colour and underline etc. Before you could format any text, you have to select it or highlight the text. You can click on the button of the actual effect you want directly from the Home Tab

6.17   **How to Select a Text**.

Click the beginning of the text and drag the mouse while holding the Left mouse button down. The text selected will be highlighted.

6.18   **How to Select a Line**

To select a line do any of the following:

1.   Position the mouse pointer at the beginning or end of the line and double click
2.   Place your cursor at the beginning of the line, hold down the shift key and press end key.
3.   Place your cursor at the beginning and drag it downward.

6.19   **How to Select a Page**

1. Position the cursor at the beginning of the page
2. Press shift down while pressing page down key

To select the whole documents Press CTRL+A

6.20 **How to Bold Text.** *Method 1*

1.   Highlight the text
2.   Click on **B** on the Home tab,

OR *Method 2.*

Highlight the text and press CTL

+B

Method 3.

1.　　Click on **Home Tab**

;2. C l i c k o n F o n t D i a l o g B o x　L a u n c h e r

3. Go to Font Style then choose **Bold.**

6.21　　**How to Centre Text.**

1.　　Click on Centre Alignment on the Home Tab

2.　　Then type, your text will be Centered OR

1.　　Highlight the text, a line or paragraph

2.　Click on Centre

Alignment Hot

Keys=CTRL+E

6.22.　　**How to Indent a Line.**

1.　Press the tab key

2.　Type the text

6.23.　　**How to Indent a Paragraph.**

1.　　Place the mouse pointer to the left of this paragraph, so that it changes into an arrow

2.　Click on the left mouse button.

3.　Click on paragraph Dialog Box Launcher under Home tab.

4.　Go to Indentation and change the value to 0.5cm for instance

5.   Click Ok

6.24.   How to Indent First Line of All Paragraph.

1.   Press the CTRL KEY AND HOLD IT DOWN
2.   Move the mouse pointer to the left side of the screen where it turns into an arrow
3.   Click once using the mouse while holding down the CTRL key.
4.   Click on paragraph dialog box Launcher under Home tab.
5.   Change the setting in the line box 0.5".
6.   Click Ok

6.25.   Changing the Font Type of Text.

1.   Select the text.
2.   Click font dialog box launcher under Home tab.
3.   Choose the desire font in the font box.
4.   Click Ok

6.26   Changing the Font Style of Text.

1.   Select the text.
2.   Click font dialog box launcher under Home tab.
3.   Click the required style in the box under front style
4.   Click Ok

6.27   Changing the Font Size of Text.

1.   Select the text
2.   Click font size list box
3.   Choose the required size in the box.

4.   Click Ok

6.28   How to Underline Texts.

1.   Select the text
2.   Click on font dialog box launcher under Home tab
3.   Click the underline style box
4.   Click the type of underline that you want
5.   Click Ok

OR highlight the text and click the U box on the formatting bar. Hot keys = CTRL +U

6.29   Changing the Colour of Text.

1.   Select the text
2.   Click the font colour list box under **Home Tab**
3.   Click the required colour 4. Click Ok
OR.
1. Select the text
2. Click the font dialog box launcher under Home tab 3. Choose the desired colour in the font colour box
    4. Click Ok.

6.30   How to Strike Line Across Text.

This is used to rule a line across the text. (e.g. ₦ or ₦)

1. Select the text
2.   Click on the font dialog box launcher
3.   Click the box in front of strike through or double strikethrough
4.   Click Ok.

6.31   Working With Superscript.

This is used to position some text above other text (e.g. A2)

1. For example, typeA2
2. Highlight 2 alone
3. Click on the font dialog box launcher
4. Click the box in front of superscript
5. Click Ok.

For subscript repeat the above step but choose subscript instead of superscript

6.32   To Add Bullet and Numbering.

1.   Type your text you want to add bullet and Numbering to or if the text is already typed, then select it (Highlight the text)
2. Go to paragraph group under **Home Tab.**
3.   Select an option by clicking on Bullet tab or Number tab
4. Click Ok.

6.34   To Delete Text.

1. Highlight the text (Your text could be a letter, word,   line, paragraph etc)
2.   Press delete key on your keyboard OR Space bar.

OR

Place your cursor at the beginning of the text and press delete key

OR

Place your cursor on the text and press CRTL+ Del keys

6.35   To Copy and Paste Text.

1.   Highlight the text you want to copy (Duplicate)

2.   Go to clipboard group under Home tab and click copy button

3.   Position your insertion point where you want the copied text to appear

4.   Click paste button on the clipboard group.

Hot keys = CTRL + C- COPY, CTRL +V
OR SHIFT+INSERT= PASTE

6.36.0 Page Layout 6.36.1 Setting up a New Document

When you begin a new document, you can start typing. MS-Word uses default settings for page size, orientation, margins, and other options. You can change these settings at any time. However, if you know from the beginning the form that you want a document to look like, it is easy to set these options before you start in order to achieve the required page set up.

6.37 Setting Margins:

Margin is the blank portion or spaces round a printed document. You can set the top, bottom, left and right margins. STEPS:

1.   Click Page Layout

2.   Click margins button

3.   Click custom margins

4.   Change the top, bottom, right and left margins using page setup dialog box.

NOTE: There are some predefined margins settings that you can choose one from.

6.38. Changing Line Spacing.

1.   Click on page layout
2.   Click on paragraph group
3.   Click on Spacing box
4.   Select whether single, 1.5, or double spacing
5.   Click on Ok

6.39   Numbering Pages.

There are two primary ways to add page numbers automatically to your document. When you add page numbers, MS-Word inserts a PAGE field into the document. When you insert a page number, MSWord puts it in the header or foot or at the top or bottom margin and aligns it in the position, which you specified either to the right side, leftside, centre, or the margins.

6.40   How to Insert Page Numbers.

METHOD 1
1.   Go to Insert Tab and click
2.   Click Page Number
3.   Choose option from the put down menu,
4.   select page number position.

METHOD 2 click the Insert bar
1.   Click header or footer
2.   Type the page number

,

NB: You can also use method 2 to include additional text with a page number, such as date or author name.

6.41   To Add a Special Effect
With drop cap command on the format you can emphasize the first letter in a paragraph

1. Highlight the character (letter)
2. Click Insert Tab
3. Click Drop Cap 4. Choose your options.
5. Click Ok

6.42   To Spell Check Your Document.

1. Open the document you want to spell check, if not displayed on your screen
2. Click on Review bar then click on Spellings Grammar OR Press F7
3. In the spelling and grammar dialog box, Computer will highlight any wrong text with a colour and the suggestion will be listed.
Click ignore to abandon your mistake pointed at, or click the correct spelling and click change.
4. Click Ok when you finish checking.

6.43   Working With Thesaurus
This is used to find synonyms and antonyms of words, it is use to improve the precision and variety of your writing Step:

1. Click Review Bar   •'
2. Click Thesaurus
3. Select the required word in the box under replace with synony

6.44.0 Newspaper Column 6.44.1 Creating Multiple Columns
Click the Column dialog box on the page layout and

then drag to select the number of columns you want. To create two or three columns of equal width select column from menu or unequal width, choose columns from menu and select the left or right preset. The Left preset makes the left column narrower than the right column, the right column preset makes the right column narrower. Then choose Ok button.

6.45. Table

A table is a grid of rows and column, each box in the grid is a cell.

6.46. To Create a New Table

1.   Position the cursor where you want to add a table

2.   On the Insert Tab click the Table Button

3.   Drag over the grid to select the size of the table you want and then release the mouse button. OR

1.   Position the insertion point where you want the table to
   appear

2. Click Table

3.   Click Insert table to bring out the Insert Table dialog box, type the number of columns and the number of rows and other options.

4.   Click Ok

6.47   Adding Text to a Table

Click in any celt. The insertion point appears next to the end of cell mark. Types as you do in any text paragraph. To move to another cell, click in it, press the TABKEY or use the arrow keys.

NB: You can add, delete, and format text in a cell just as you would in any paragraph or text.

6.48   Split a Cell into Multiple Cells in a Table.

1,   On the Tables and Borders toolbar, click Draw Table.

2, The pointer changes to a pencil.

3, Drag the pencil to create new cell partitions.

Tip To split multiple cells, select them, and then click Split Cells.

6.49   Split a Table or Insert Text Before a Table

1.   To split a table in two, click the row that you want to be the first row of the second table.
2.   To insert text before a table, click the first row of the table.

On the Table menu, click Split Table.

6.50   changing the Position of Text in a Table.

Changing the orientation of text by default, Microsoft Word aligns text horizontally in table cells, callouts, text boxes, or AutoShapes. You can change the text orientation so that the text is displayed vertically.

Changing the alignment of text in a table cell by default, Word aligns text in a table to the upper left of a cell. You can change the alignment of text in a cell both the vertical alignment (top, centre, or bottom) and the horizontal alignment (left, centre, or right).

NB: When you select two rows and click the insert row button M5Word inserts two new rows above the selected rows. To add a row to the end of the table, click in the last cell of the table and press TAB. To add a column to the end of the table, position point outside the last column, choose select column from the Table menu, and then choose insert column.

6.51   Sorting Table.

1.   Select the Table.

2.   Click Home Tab.

3.   Click Sort menu, Sort Dialog box appears.

6.52   Type and Move Around in a Table.

Press	To
The TAB key anywhere in a table except at the end of the last row	Move to the next cell
The TAB key at the end of the last row	Add a new row at the bottom of the table
SHIFT+TAB	Move to the preceding cell
UP ARROW or DOWN ARROW	Move to the preceding or next row
ALT+HOME, or ALT+7 on the numeric keypad (NUM LOCK must be off)	Move to the first cell in the row
ALT+END or ALT+1onthe numeric keypad (NUM LOCK must be off)	Move to the last cell in the row
ALT+PAGE UP, or ALT+9 on the numeric keypad	Move to the first cell in the column

(NUM LOCK must be off)	
ALT+PAGE DOWN, or ALT + 3 on the numeric keypad (NUM LOCK must be off)	Move to the last cell in the column
ENTER at the beginning of the first cell	Start a new paragraph Add text before a table at the beginning of a document

6.53. Working With Graphics/Pictures.

6.54. Displaying a Text Box.

1. Place your cursor in the insertion point. 2. Click the text box on the insert bar

3.   Choose the text box option.

4.   Move the cursor inside the box you have just drawn and click 5. Type any text and format it.

6.55   Drawing Circle.

1.   Click on the shape dialog box on Insert bar.

2.   Click the box with the circle sign.

3.   Move the cursor to the point where you want to place the object

4.   Click and hold the mouse button

5.   Drag until you are satisfied

6.   Then release the mouse

6.56   How to Insert Picture/Clip Art

1. Click the point where you want to place the picture
2. Click the insert tab
3. Go to illustrations group
4. Click on Picture/Clip Art, the dialog box appears,
5. Select the required Picture /clipart by double clicking on it.

6.57 WordArt

With Word Art, you can create interesting text effects to enhance the documents. After creating a word Art, you can enclose it in a frame and add borders, resize it and move it.

To change the text or text effects of a word Art object at any time, just double-click it.

6.58. How to Create a New WordArt.

1. Position the insertion point where you want to add a word Art
2. Click insert tab
3. Go to text group
4. Click WordArt
5. In the WordArt dialog box, select an option (Text effect option)
   (Word display the text entry)
6. In the text entry box, type the text you want to format (You can format your text in this box).
7. Click Ok when you have finished creating the text effect
8. (The text is inserted into the document)

6.59.0 Printing

It is a good idea to always preview your documents before sending it to the printer, this will enable you to see how it will look on the paper.

6.59.1 To Preview a Document
1.   Open the file you want to preview before printing if it is not yet displayed on your screen.
2.   Click print on **file menu.**
3.   Choose Print Preview under preview and print the document
4.   To exit print preview and return to the previous view of the document, click the close button.

6.60 Printing a Document
1.   Click print on **File Menu**
2.   In the print dialog box, you can select from several printing options Copies page range, printer, etc.
3.   Click **OK.**

REVIEW QUESTIONS
1.   Explain Word Processing in detail.
2.   Explain how the following can be achieved:
a.   Password a saved file
b.   Creating a table with 6 column and 10 rows
c.   Printing of pages 2 to 7 of document of 20 pages
3.   Explain how to print a document on the flash drive.
4.   What is the difference between **Save** and

Save As, **close** and **quit** in Microsoft word.

5.   Explain step by step how you can retrieve a file from a flash and save it on the hard disk with a different name.

6.   Mention and explain the uses of Tabs in Microsoft.

MODULE FOUR

In this module you will learn the following:

- Features of CorelDraw.
- How to start CorelDraw.
- CorelDraw terminology and concept.
- Using the Tools in CorelDraw.
- How to create Logo, Letterhead, Complimentary card etc.
- How to apply perspective.
- Printing in CorelDraw.
- Image Capturing Device.
- Scanning.
- File formats.

CHAPTER SEVEN

7.0.   Coreldraw

7.1.   Introduction to CorelDraw

CorelDRAW is an intuitive graphics design application that helps designers to create powerful advertisement materials like bill board, posters, complimentary cards etc, it is also a vital tool in the design of a web.

It is a comprehensive vector-based drawing and graphic-design package for the graphics professional, marketers, web designers, architects, teachers etc. ‚‚

There are versions of CorelDraw but the knowledge of one version can be used to work in others. The features of higher (new) versions are always more than the lower (old) ones.

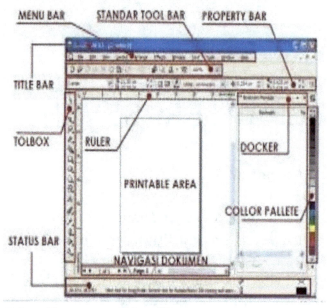

7.2. Features of CorelDraw.

Fig 7.0

7.2

Title Bar

Fig 7.0

The First Bar on the screen is called the Title Bar, where the name of the document appears. Coreldraw18 – C: \jose.crd

7.3 Menu Bar

fig 7.1

Next to the title bar is the Menu bar, which includes the following menus. File, Edit, View, Layout. Arrange. Effect, Bitmaps, Text, Tools, Window ana Help. Each of these has its own function.

Standard Tool bar

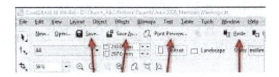

fig 7.2

The standard toolbar is a shortcut menu where each action is represented with an Icon or button e.g. New, Open, Save, Print, Cut, Copy, Paste, Undo, Redo, Import, Export etc. Most of these buttons represent what you use your menus in the menu bar to do often. What these buttons represent wilt be revealed as the pointer is placed on them.

Property Bar

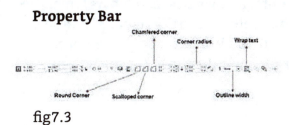

fig7.3

Property Bar is used in editing of text, bitmaps and OLE Objects.

Status Bar

The last bar at the bottom of the CorelDraw window is the Status Bar as seen in fig 7.0 above where the current status of the objects and characters are displayed. Status Bar shows size of the object, the colour, the layer, the font etc. It also describes what each menu does on clicking them.

Drawing Page

The portion of a drawing window enclosed by a rectangle with a shadow effect.

This is an area in which the drawing and the typesetting are done, only characters and objects that appear on the page will be printed.

fig 7.5

Horizontal and Vertical Scroll Bars

There are also horizontal and vertical scroll bars which allow you to move the document to the right or left and up or down respectively to view parts of the work that are not displayed within your document layout screen.

fig 7.6

NOTE: There are some other bars that you need to

activate before they can appear. Do this by placing your arrow on menu bar, right click and choose the bar you need.

Rulers

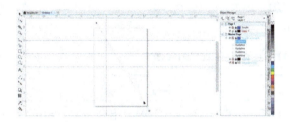

fig 7.7

The rulers allow you take accurate measurement of your drawing especially when drawing to specification is needed.

Tool Box

This toolbox as seen in fig 7.0 contains tools that are used in drawing different shapes, giving colour to objects, special effects etc.

Colour Palette

A collection of solid colours from which you can choose colours for fills and outlines. See fig. 7.0

7.3 Starting with CorelDraw
There are three methods of starting CorelDraw
Method One:
    i. Click on Start

ii. Click on CorelDraw
icon

Method Two:
Double Click on the CorelDraw Icon on the
desktop.

Method Three:
i.   Click on document folder on
the **task bar** ii.   search for the
file and click*(this is used to open
existing documents).*

7.4 CorelDraw Terminology and Concept

Term	Description
Object	An element in a drawing such as an image, shape, line, text, curve, symbol, or layer.
Drawing	The work you create in CorelDraw: for example, custom artwork, logos, posters, and newsletters
Vector Graphic	An image generated from mathematical descriptions that determine the position, length, and direction in which lines are
Bitmap	drawn.An image composed of grids of pixels or dots
Docker	A window containing available commands and settings relevant to a specific tool or task
Flyout	A button that opens a group of related tools or menu items
Artistic text	A type of text to which you can apply special effects, such as shadows

Paragrap h Text	A type of text to which you can apply formatting options, and which can be edited in large blocks
Pixel	A colored dot that is the smallest part of a bitmap.
Point	A unit of measure used primarily in typesetting to define type sizes. There are approximately 72 points to an inch and 1 2 points to a pica.

Table 7.0

7.5 Using the toolbar to start a drawing

The toolbar displays by default and contains buttons that are shortcuts to many of the menu commands,

1. On the toolbar, click the **New button** to start a new drawing. By default, this creates a drawing page with a width of 8.5 inches and a height of 11 inches.
2. From the Zoom levels list box, choose To height.
This fits the height of the drawing page inside the drawing window. 3. On the toolbar click on **Open button** to open an existing file.
4. Click on other buttons on the toolbar and see the effect.

NOTE: Before we move further go to the tool box and place your arrow on each tool their names will be reveal to you. Also, click on each tool to see the Flyout menu?

7.6.0 Using a Flyout Tool to Draw

7.6.1 To draw a rectangle by specifying width and height

i.   Open the Rectangle flyout, and click

the 4 point rectangle tool.

ii.　　　　On drawing page, click and drag to size 40 X 40 millimeters/ then release the mouse button,

NOTE: *As you draw and drag the size (width and height) of the object is shown at the status bar*

7.7　Using the Property Bar to Specify the Size of an Object

The property bar is a bar with commands that relate to an active tool. For example, when you click the 4 point rectangle tool, the property bar displays commands relevant to creating and editing rectangles.

1 Specify the following dimensions in the Object(s) size boxes on the property bar:

width 40

height 40

2 Click in the drawing page. It is easier to specify accurately the size of the object using the second method

Note: *To take a closer look at an object, choose the Zoom tool from the Zoom flyout tool in the toolbox. Click the object to zoom in. Right-click the object to zoom out.*

7.8　Using the Color Palette to Add Colour to Your Drawings

1. Select the rectangle drawn by using the pick tool　2. Go to color palette and click a desired color.

repeat the above procedure for ellipse tool smart tool and basic tool.

7.9 Using the Freehand tool to Draw a Curve Line.

1. Click on the Freehand tool
2. Click and drag to a desired length then release the button.
3. Click on the Shape tool, then click on the line drawn
4. Convert Line To Curve tool will be activated
5. Click on the Convert Line To Curve
6. Click on any of the nodes and use it to change the line to curve

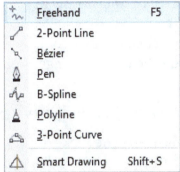

	Freehand	F5
	2-Point Line	
	Bézier	
	Pen	
	B-Spline	
	Polyline	
	3-Point Curve	
	Smart Drawing	Shift+S

fig 7.8

7.10 Using the Outline Tool to Increase/Decrease the Width of a Line.

1. Draw a line.

2. Go to Outline tool, select each of the tool from hairline to last one and see how each works. Then later choose No outline tool.

3. Then click on the Outline Pen Dialog
4. Choose different colors, widths, styles to see how they work

7.11   Working With Text

There are two types of text in CorelDraw namely; *artistic* text and *paragraph text*. Artistic text is used for short blocks of text that can have effects applied to them, whereas paragraph text is used for larger blocks of text that can be extensively formatted just as if you are in a word processing package.

1. In the toolbox, click the Text tool.
2. Click on the page, and type Sileola. The word Sileola displays in artistic text.
3. Click the Text tool, drag to create a paragraph text frame, and type Sileoja. The word Sileola displays now in paragraph text.
4. In the toolbox, click the Pick tool.
5. Click outside the drawing page. This deselects all objects.

7.12 How to Edit Text Properties Using the Property Bar

1. Select the word Sileola using the Pick tool.
2. From the Font list list box on the property bar, choose Verdana.
3. From the Font size list box, choose
4. Click the Italic button on the property bar.
5. If the text moves off the page, reposition it by using the Pick tool to select the object and drag it.
6. Select the paragraph text frame using the Pick tool.
7. From the Font list list box, choose Verdana.
8. In the Font size list box, type 30.
9. Click outside the drawing page.

7.13 Adding Colour to Your Text Using Color Palette

1. Click on the Text tool A
2. Type lreOluwa
3. Click on the Pick toot
4. Go to color palette and choose a color.
5. Click outside the drawing page to deselect the object.

7.14 Layers in CorelDraw

Coreldraw draw objects in layers i.e. two objects can be placed on one another, one will be in layer one and the second object will be in layer two. The position of the objects can also be rearranged.

To demonstrate this

1. Draw a circle using the Elipse tool
2. Fill it with blue using the color palette,
3. Type OPE
4. Click on the Pick tool
5. Go to the Color and choose color red
6. Go to the font list box and choose Black Arial
7. Click on the text (OPE)
8. Click and hold down the button to carry the text,

drop the text on the circle.

The result will look like this:

Using the knowledge of the tools learnt above let us apply it to do some exercises.

7.15 Creating a Business Card:

Exercise One

a. Measure the width with ruler guide (3.0 inches)
b. Measure the height with ruler guide (2.0 inches)
c. Type the name and designation *(with artistic text)* at. desired position
d. Draw the logo of the company or organization and placed at a desired position
e. Type the address, phone number *(with artistic text)* and place them at a desired position.

Note: *there may be a border round the card or it may be left opened.*

fig

7.18

The above complementary card is a sample your own may be different.

7.16 Letterhead
Exercise Two.

a. Type the name of organization (preferably on A4 size paper)
b. Insert the logo at the appropriate position
c. Type the services render by the company

d.   Type the address, telephone number

E. Type website and email (if any)

fig .20

NOTE: There *is no fixed rule for the design of a letter head or ID card but make sure you are passing the right message to the those who will see the design.*

7.17 ID Cards

Exercise three

There are various ways of creating an Id cards but the following steps are common:

a.   Type the name of the organization (*may be the 1st of the last on the ID card*)

b.   Inset the logo

c.   Type the name of the owner

d.   Type the designation

e.   Create a place to insert the owner's picture

f.   Create a place to sign

g.   At the back type the address of where to return the ID card if found.

h.   Type the validity date.

i.   Create where the head of the organization will sign.

7.18   How to Create Logo

A   *fig 7.21*   B -*fig 7.22*

C- *fig 7.23*

How the above logos were created wilt be explained in detail.

During the explanation you will learn the following;

Fit text to path, Duplication, Rotation, Grouping.

7.19   To Create Logo A Above, the Procedure Below Should be Followed:

Step 1
1.   Go to ellipse tool and click
2.   Click on the drawing page drag to draw a circle of width=130mm x height=130mm.
3.   Type IRE COMPUTER TECHNOLOGY
4.   Click the Circle and the typed text "IRE'
COMPUTER TECHNOLOGY"
5.   Go to the Text Menu and click on Fit Text to Path Menu

6.   Go to the distance from path tool and specify the distance of the text from the circle.
2.   Type ijebu ode.
3.   Select both the ijebu ode typed and the circle
4.   Go to fit text to path and click.
5.   Click on text placement to place the text down
6.   Click on the arrange menu and choose break text apart
7.   Draw another lager circle
8.   Click on the larger circle and click on arrange
9.   Click on order and choose sent to back
10. Click on the outer circle and fill it with color
11. Draw another lager circle
12. Click on the larger circle and click on arrange
13. Click on order and choose sent to back
14. Click on the outer circle and fill it with color

Step 2

1.   Click on the inner circle and fill it with color as above

2.   Click on the Text tool

3.   Type I and go to font list box to change the font 4. Repeat the same for C and T; choosing the font above.

The procedure for logo C is almost the same as that of Logo A

In Logo B,
Follow this procedure

1.   Draw a triangle using Bezier tool or Smart tool

2.   Click on the triangle and Duplicate using Control + D

3.   Click on one of the duplicated triangle twice

4.   Rotate using one of the arrow nodes

5.   Place the triangle on top of the other

6.   Fill the two triangle with color

7.   Click on the upper triangle and change the outline to white

8.   Add the text on top

7.20   Three-Dimensional

You can create the illusion of three-dimensional depth in CorelDraw objects by adding contour, perspective, extrusion, or drop-shadow effects.

Contouring Objects:

1   Open the Interactive Tools Flyout, and click the Interactive Contour Tool.

2   Click an object or a set of grouped objects and drag the start handle toward the centre to create an inside contour.

3   Move the slider to change the number of

contour steps.

7.21   Applying Perspective to Objects:
You can create a perspective effect by shortening one or two sides of an object. This effect gives an object the appearance of receding in one or two directions, thereby creating a one-point perspective or a two-point perspective.

You can add a perspective effect to objects or grouped objects. However, you can't add a perspective effect to paragraph text; bitmapped images; linked groups, such as contours, blends, extrusions; and objects created with the Artistic media tool.

After you apply a perspective effect, you can copy it to other objects in your drawing, and you can remove it from the object.

7.22   To Apply a Two-Point Perspective
1   Select an object.
2   Click Effects go to Add perspective.
3   Drag two nodes to apply the effect you want.

7.23   To Apply a One-Point Perspective 1 Select an object.
2   Click Effects Add perspective.
3   Hold down CTRL, and drag a node.

The Results will look like these:

7.24 Creating Drop Shadows

a.   Use an Artistic Text to Type

    b.   Go to interactive drop shadow tool and click

    c.   Then place your cursor on the objects and drag.

The result will look like the followings:

7.25   Interactive Transparency Tool

1. Draw and Select an object
2. Go to the Interactive **Transparency Tool** and click
3. Click and drag the nodes
4. Go to **transparency type** and change the type of the transparency
5. On the property bar change the property of the object and see how the tool works.

7.26.0 Printing.

It is advisable to always preview your document before printing.

This will enable you to see how I twill look like on the paper.

To print, do the following: »

    a.   click on the Print Preview under the File Menu

    b.   If you are satisfied with the document, you previewed click on Print This Sheet Now under the File Menu to print the current page.

    c.   To print all the documents (i.e, all the pages) if you have more than one page, go to Print under the File menu and click.

    d.   If you are not satisfied with the documents click on Close Print Preview to go back and adjust it.

7.26.1 Print Setup

If you have more than one printer drivers installed on your computer system please choose the appropriate one before sending your document to the printer. To choose the appropriate printer, follow these steps.

a.   Go to Print Setup under the File Menu

b.   Choose the appropriate printer (i.e. the driver meant for the printer you want to use.

c.   Go to properties and click.

d.   Choose the appropriate options like the orientation, numbers of copies etc

OR In the Print Preview window

a.   Go to the status bar and click on the printer icon

b.   List of the available printers are given, then choose the printer you want to use.

To print on the letter head
Follow these steps

a.   Measure the distance between the top edge of the paper and a little below the last line of the letters (i.e. the design on the head of the paper).

b.   If the measurement taken on the letterhead is 2 inches for example, on the paste board let your design start from the 2 inches measured on the paper.

NOTE: make sure you use the same unit of

measurement (i.e if you use inches of centimeter

on the paper, use the same on the pasteboard).

7.27.   Color Separation

Colour separation enables you to print each colour you have on the documents in a separate sheet. We have four primary colours in coreldraw; black, yellow, magenta and cyan. If you have up to six colours the primary colours will be mixed by the computer to form the two other colours to make up for the six colours. For example, mixture of black, magenta, and yellow will form brown, yellow and cyan will form green etc.

To separate colours, take the following steps. a. Click on **Print Preview** under file menu

b. Click on **Separations** under **Settings**, the print options dialogue box is displayed.
c. Go to **Print Separations** and click
d. Click on apply button, then click OK.
e. Load the printer with the right paper and print.

REVIEW QUESTIONS

1. State three differences between CorelDraw and Microsoft Word 2. Prepare a logo using the following objects:
a. A flying bird
b. Two circles
c. The name of a company
3. Use three letter to design a logo of your choice.
4. Prepare a complimentary card.
5. Prepare a birthday greeting card.
6. Explain Colour Separation
7. What are the steps to take in printing a document on flash drive?

CHAPTER EIGHT

8.0   IMAGE CAPTURING AND SCANNING

8.1   What is Image Capturing?

Image capturing is the receding and storage of image in the computer memory or as computer file using device attached or embedded to the computer system. The image captured can later be edited or burn on the CD. The image capturing devices also snap pictures which can be edited, printed or used as part of another document. Examples of these devices are webcam which may either be embedded to your computer (especially the laptop) or attached to your desktop computer, digital camera, phone camera etc. The image captured or snapped by these devices can be downloaded to your computer system and saved in a folder, but an embedded webcam automatically saved the files in a specially created folder.

Fig 8.0

8.2 Scanner

A scanner is an input -device that uses optical lens to scan documents, translating the pattern of light and dark (or colour) into a digital signal that can be manipulated by either optical character recognition software or graphics software.

8.3 Types of Scanning Machines:

The most common type of scanner is flatbed. The flatbed scanner looks like a common office photocopy machine, documents are placed face down on its flat piece of glass. This set of scanner can scan a wide area of a document at a time e.g. Quarto, A4, Legal, B5 papers etc.

ii. Another type of scanner is the hand scanner, this is becoming less popular for scanning documents into the system because of its disadvantages. The user holds it in his hand and drag it over the document. Hand scanner cannot scan more than a few inches wide at a time. The image may tilt to one side, if not properly handled.

Android phone with appropriate software can be used to scan document and latter send it to the computer system.

NOTE: How to use a scanner depends on the instructions or help information from the manufacturer but the following information can help you in operating your scanner.

8.4   How To Scan Step A:

i.   Make sure your scanner is connected properly

before switching your system on.

ii.   Place the document to be scanned face down in the   upper right corner of the scanner glass.

iii.   Press the Scanner button to activate the Scanner   software.

OR Click on the Icon of the scanner software on the desktop.

Step B:
   i.   Choose Scanning options in the scanner software.
   ii. Select a destination from the Scan,
   iii. Keep the Selected Parts of Page or View Page First box checked if you want to see a view area.

   Document can be scanned as PDF, document or Jpeg

MODULE FIVE

In this module you will learn the following:

Introduction to Microsoft Excel
How to use the Ribbon
The Formula Bar
The Status Bar
How to Move around the Worksheet
Editing in Excel
Excel Formula and Data
Cell Addressing
How to Create
Charts
Printing in Excel

CHAPTER NINE

9.0   MICROSOFT EXCEL

9.1 Introduction to Excel

Microsoft Excel is an electronic spreadsheet that displays numerical data in cells in a simulated accountant's worksheet of rows and columns in which hidden formulas can perform calculations on the visible data. Changing the contents of one cell can cause automatic recalculation of other cells.

There are versions of Microsoft Excel e.g. Excel 2005, 2007, 2016 etc. the new versions are always more sophisticated than the old versions.

9.2 The Microsoft Excel Window

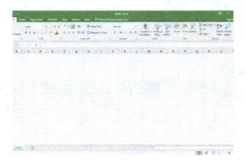

fig 9.0

The excel window consists of Ribbons and commands, the ribbon is used is arranging the commands into groups while the command are used to tell the Excel package what to do.

9.3 The Ribbon

The Ribbon above is somehow similar to the ribbon in Microsoft Word but there are differences for instance in Excel we have Formula, Data, Add-ins which are not included in Microsoft Word.

9.4 Worksheets

Fig. 9.2

Microsoft Excel consists of worksheets. Each worksheet contains columns and rows. The columns are lettered A to Z and then continuing with AA, AB, AC and so on; the rows are numbered 1 to 1,048,576. The number of columns and rows you can have in a worksheet is limited by your computer memory and your system resources.

The combination of a column coordinate and a row coordinate make up a cell address. For example, the cell located in the upper-left corner of the worksheet is cell A1, meaning column A, row 1, Cell E10 is located under column E on row 10. Data are entered into the cells on the worksheet.

9.5 The Formula Bar

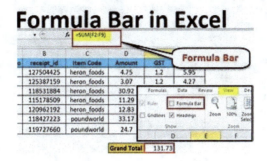

Fig 9.3

Formula Bar When the Formula bar is turned on, the cell address of the cell you are in displays in the Name box which is located on the left side of the Formula bar. Cell entries display on the right side of the Formula bar. If you do not see the Formula bar in your window, perform the following steps:

1. Choose the View tab.

2. Click Formula Bar in the Show/Hide group. The Formula bar appears.

Note: The current cell address displays on the left side of the Formula bar.

9.6 The Status Bar

Year	Chrome	IE	Firefox	Safari	Other	
2012	33.23	33.74	24.15	6.17	2.71	
2013	42.63	29.25	20.82	4.84	2.46	
2014	48.78	23.19	19.57	5	3.46	
2015	54.37	18.88	17.54	5.06	4.15	
2016	61.18	12.11	15.45	4.79	6.47	

Fig 9.4

The Status bar appears at the very bottom of the Excel window and provides such information as the sum, average, minimum, and maximum value of selected numbers. You can change what displays on the Status bar by right-clicking on the Status bar and selecting the options you want from the Customize Status Bar menu. You click a menu item to select it. You click it again to deselect it. A check mark next to an item means the item is selected.

9.7 Move Around a Worksheet

By using the arrow keys, you can move around your worksheet. You can use the down arrow key to move downward one cell at a time. You can use the up arrow key to move upward one cell at a time. You can use the Tab key to move across the page to the right, one cell at a time. You can hold down the Shift key and then press the Tab key to move to the left, one cell at a time. You can use the right and left arrow keys to move right or left one cell at a. time. The Page Up and Page Down keys move up and down one page at a time. If you hold down the Ctrl key and then press the Home key, you move to the beginning of the worksheet.

9.8 Move Around the Worksheet

Exercise 1

The Down Arrow Key
Press the down arrow key several times. Note that the cursor Moves downward one cell at a time.

The Up Arrow Key
Press the up arrow key several times. Note that the cursor moves upward one cell at a time.

The Tab Key
Move to cell A1.

1.   Press the Tab key several times. Note that the cursor moves to the right one celt at a time.

The Shift+Tab Keys

>   Hold down the Shift key and then press Tab. Note that the cursor moves to the Left one cell at a time.

The Right and Left Arrow Keys

1.   Press the right arrow key several times. Note that the cursor moves to the right.

2. Press the left arrow key several times. Note that the cursor moves to the left.

Page Up and Page Down

>   1.   Press the Page Down key. Note that the cursor moves down one page.

>   2.   Press the Page Up key. Note that the cursor moves up one page.

The Ctrl-Home Key

>   1.   Move the cursor to column J.

2.   Stay in column J and move the cursor to row 20.

3.   Hold down the Ctrl key while you press the Home key. Excel moves to cell A1.

Go To Cells Quickly

The following are shortcuts for moving quickly from one cell in a worksheet to a cell in a different part of the worksheet. Exercise 2

Go To Key -- F5

The F5 function key is the "Go To" key. If you press the F5 key, you are prompted for the cell to which you wish to go. Enter the cell address, and the cursor jumps to that cell.

1.   Press F5. The Go To dialog box opens.

2.   Type J3 in the Reference field.

3.   Press Enter. Excel moves to cell J3.

Goto--Ctrl+G   *

You can also use Ctrl+G to go to a specific cell.

1.   Hold down the Ctrl key while you press "g" (Ctrl+g). The Go To dialog box opens.

2.   Type C4 in the Reference field.

3.   Press Enter. Excel moves to cell C4.

9.9 The Name Box

You can also use the Name box to go to a specific cell. Just type the cell you want to go to in the Name box and then press Enter.

1.   Type C11 in the Name box.

2.   Press Enter. Excel moves to cell C11.

Select Cells

If you wish to perform a function on a group of cells, you must first select those cells by highlighting them. The exercises that follow teach you how to select.

Exercise 3

9.10   How To Select Cells

To select cells A1 to E1:

1.   Go to cell A1.
2.   Press the F8 key. This anchors the cursor,
3.   Note that "Extend Selection" appears on the Status bar in the lower-left corner of the window. You are in the Extend mode.
4.   Click in cell E7. Excel highlights cells A1 to E7.
5.   Press Esc and click anywhere on the worksheet to clear the highlighting.   .   i

9.11   Alternative Method: Select Cells by Dragging

You can also select an area by holding down the left mouse button and dragging the mouse over the area. In addition, you can select noncontiguous areas of the worksheet by doing the following:

1.   Go to cell A1.
2.   Hold down the Ctrl key. You won't release it until step 9. Holding down the Ctrl key enables you to select noncontiguous areas of the worksheet.
3.   Press the left mouse button.
4.   While holding down the left mouse button, use the mouse to move from cell A1 toC5.
5.   Continue to hold down the Ctrl key, but release the left mouse button.
6.   Using the mouse, place the cursor in cell

07.

7.   Press the left mouse button.

8.   While holding down the left mouse button, move to cell F10. Release the left mouse button.

9.   Release the Ctrl key. Cells A1 to C5 and cells D7 to F10 are selected.

10.   Press Esc and click anywhere on the worksheet to remove the highlighting.

9.12   How To Enter Data In Excel

In this section, you will learn how to enter data into your worksheet. First, place the cursor in the cell in which you want to start entering data. Type some data, and then press Enter. If you need to delete, press the Backspace key to delete one character at a time.

Exercise 4

How To Enter Data

Fig 9.6

1.   Place the cursor in cell A1.

2.   Type Josephine. Do not press Enter at this time.

9.13   How To Edit Cell

After you enter data into a cell, you can edit the data by pressing F2 while you are in the cell you wish to edit.

9.14 Edit a Cell

Exercise 5
Change "Jossy"
to "Josephine." '1.
Move to cell A1.
2.   Press F2.
3.   Use the Backspace key to delete the "sy" .
4.   Type ephine.
5.   Press Enter.

9.15 Alternate Method: Editing a Cell by Using the Formula Bar

You can also edit the cell by using the Formula ban You change "Jossy" to "Josephine" in the following exercise.

1.   Move the cursor to cell A1.
2.   Click in the formula area of the Formula bar. 3. Use the backspace key to erase the "sy."
4.   Type ephine.
5.   Press Enter.

9.16   Change a Cell Entry
Typing in a cell replaces the old cell entry with the new information you type.

1.   Move the cursor to cell A1.
2.   Type Ayo.
3.   Press Enter. The name "Ayo" replaces "Josephine."

9.17   How to Wrap Text Long Text

A typed text may be too long to fit in the cell, the text then overlaps the next cell. If you do not want it to overlap the next cell, you can wrap the text.

Exercise 6

Wrap Text Move to cell A2.

1.   Type Text too long.

2.   Press Enter.

3.   Return to cell A2.

4.   Choose the Home tab. .

5.   Click the Wrap Text button. Excel wraps the text

in the cell.

9.18   How to Delete a Cell Entry

To delete an entry in a cell or a group of cells, you place the cursor in the cell or select the group of cells and press Delete. Exercise 7 Delete a Cell Entry 1. Select cells A1 toA2.

2. Press the Delete key.

9.19 How to Close Excel

To Close Microsoft Excel.

1.   Click the file menu.

2.   Search for Close and click. Excel closes.

9.20.0 Entering Excel Formulas and Formatting

Data 9.20.1 Set the Enter Key Direction

In Microsoft Excel, you tell the cursor how to move when you press the Enter key. You can use the Direction box in the Excel Options pane to set the cursor movement (i.e up, down, left, right), or not at all. Perform the steps that follow to set the cursor to move down when you press the Enter key.

1.   Click the file menu. A menu appears.

2.   Click Excel Options in the lower-right corner. The Excel Options pane appears.

Click Advanced.

3.   If the check box next to After Pressing Enter

Move Selection is not checked, click the box to check it.

4.   If Down does not appear in the Direction box, click the down arrow next to the' Direction box and then click Down.

5.   Click OK. Excel sets the Enter direction to down.

9.21   Perform Mathematical Calculations

When entering a mathematical formula, precede the formula with an equal sign. Use the following to indicate the type of calculation you wish to perform:

+ Addition

- Subtraction   *

* Multiplication

/ Division

^ Exponential

9.22   Addition.

1.   Type 3 in cell A1.

2.   Press Enter. Excel moves down one cell.

3.   Type 6 in cell A2.

4.   Press Enter. Excel moves down one cell.

5.   Type =A1+A2 in cell A3.

6.   Click the check mark on the Formula bar. Excel adds cell A1 to cell A2 and displays the result in cell A3. The formula displays on the Formula bar.

Note: Clicking the check mark on the Formula bar is similar to pressing Enter. Excel records your entry but does not move to the
next cell.

9.23 Subtraction

Type 8 in cell A3.

1. Press Enter. Excel moves

down one cell. 2. Type 6 in

cell A4._

3.   Press Enter. Excel moves down one cell.

4.   Type =A3-A4 in cell A5.

5.   Click the check mark on the Formula bar. Excel subtracts cell A4 from cell A3 and the result displays in cell A5. The formula displays on the Formula bad

9.24 Multiplication

1.   Move to Cell D4

2.   Type **Multiply.**

3.   Press Enter. Excel moves down one cell.

4.   Type 2 in cell C2.

5.   Press Enter. Excel moves down one cell.

6.   Type 3 in cell C3.

7.   Press Enter. Excel moves down one cell.

8.   Type =C2*C3 in cell C4.

9.   Click the check mark on the Formula bar. Excel multiplies C1 by cell C2 and displays the result in cell C3. The formula displays on the Formula bar

9.25

Division 1.

Press F5.

2.   Type D1 in the Reference field.

3.   Press Enter. Excel moves to cell D1.

4.   Type Divide.

5.   Press Enter. Excel moves down one cell.

6.   Type 6 in cell D2.

7.   Press Enter. Excel moves down one cell.

8.   Type 3 in cell D3.

9. Press Enter. Excel moves down one celt.

10. Type =D2/D3 in cell D4.

11. Click the check mark on the Formula bar. Excel divides cell D2 by cell D3 and displays the result in cell D4. The formula displays on the Formula bar.

9.26 Creating Formulas

When creating formulas, you can reference cells and include numbers. All of the following formulas are valid:

=A2/B2

=A1+12-B3

=A2*B2+12

=24+53

9.27 AutoSum

You can use the AutoSum button *Mon* the Home tab to automatically add a column or row of numbers. When you press the AutoSum button. Excel selects the numbers it thinks you want to add. If you then click the check mark on the Formula bar or press the Enter key, Excel adds the numbers. If Excel's guess as to which numbers you want to add is wrong, you can select the cells you want.

AutoSum

Exercise 8

The following illustrates AutoSum:

1. Go to cell A1.

2. Type 4.5

3. Press Enter. Excel moves down one cell.

4. Type 6.

5.   Press Enter. Excel moves down one cell.

6.   Type 8.

7.   Press Enter.

8.   Type 0.5.

9.   Type 8.

10.   Click on cell A1 and drag to highlight from AI to A5 .

11.   Click the AutoSum button in the Editing group. Excel adds Cells AI through A5 and displays the result in cell A6.

1.   Type Peju in Cell A1, Ayomide in Cell 1, Ire in Cell C1, Pelumi in Cell
        D1 and Feranmi in cell E1.

2.   Select cellsA1toE1.

3.   Choose the Home tab.

4.   Click the Center button in the Alignment group. Excel centers each cell's content.

9.30 Left-Align

To left-align cells AI to E1:

1.   Select cells A1 to E1.

2.   Choose the Home tab.

3.   Click the Align Text Left button in the
        Alignment group. Excel left-aligns each
        cell's content.

9.31 Right-Align

To right-align cells A1 to El:

1.   Select cells A1 to E1. Click in cell A1.

2.   Choose the Home tab.

3.   Click the Align Text Right button. Excel

right-aligns the cell's content.

4.   Click anywhere on your worksheet to clear the highlighting.

9.32   How To Perform Advanced Mathematical Calculations

Precedence is very important in Excel, calculations are performed from left to right, with multiplication and division performed before addition and subtraction.

9.33   Advanced Calculations

Exercise 10

1.   Move to cell A1.

2.   Type $=7+3+12/2*4$.

3.   Press Enter

Note: In the above exercise division operation is perform first (i.e.12/2), followed by multiplication (i.e.6*4) 7 is added to the answer, and then 3. The answer, 34, appears in cell A1.

Parentheses can be used to change the order of calculation. Microsoft Excel calculates the information in parentheses first.

1.   Double-click in cell A1.

2.   Edit the cell to read $= (7+3+12)/2*4$.

3.   Press Enter.

Note: Microsoft Excel adds 7 plus 3 plus 12, divides the answer by 2, and then multiplies the result by 4. The answer, 44, displays in cell A1.

9.34 Copy, Cut, Paste, and Cell Addressing

In Excel, data can be copied from one area of a worksheet to another or to another worksheet.

Cell addresses in formulas are recorded in three

different ways, namely *absolute, relative,* and mixed. With relative cell addressing, when copying a formula from one area of the worksheet to another, Excel records the position of the cell relative to the cell that originally contained the formula. With *absolute* cell addressing, Excel references the same cells, no matter where you copy the formula. Mixed cell addressing can be used to keep the row constant while the column changes, or vice versa. The following exercises demonstrate.

Exercise 11

Copy, Cut, Paste, and Cell Addressing

9.35   How to Copy with the Ribbon

1.   Type Toyin in Cell A1
2.   Select Cell A1 by clicking on it
3.   Choose the Home tab.
4.   Click the Copy button in the Clipboard group.
5.   Take your cursor to cell E11
6.   Click the Paste button in the Clipboard group.
7.   Press the Esc key to exit the Copy mode.

9.36 Copy with the Context Menu

1   Go to Cell A9 and type 12. Press Enter
2.   lnCellA10Type14
3.   Select cellsA9toA10 by clicking on A9,
4.   Press and hold the Shift key down and press down arrow key once.
5.   Release the shift key and Right-click. A context menu and a Mini toolbar appear.
6.   Click Copy, which is located on the context menu.
7.   Move to cell C4.
8.   Right-click. A context menu appears,

9.   Click Paste. Excel copies the contents of cells A9 to A10 to cells C4 to C5.

10.   Press Esc to exit Copy mode.

9.37 Absolute Cell Addressing

Using the F4 key a cell address can be made an absolute by placing a dollar sign in front of the row and column identifiers.

1.   Go to cell D13.

2.   Type =

3.   Click cell E10.

4.   Press F4. Dollar signs appear before the E and the 10.

5.   Type +.

6.   Click cell F1.

7.   Press F4. Dollar signs appear before the F and the 1.

8.   Type*.

9.   Click cell G11.

10.   Press F4. Dollar signs appear before the G and the 11.

11.   Click the check mark on the formula bar. Excel records the formula in cell D13.

9.38 Mixed Cell Addressing

You use mixed cell addressing to reference a cell when you want to copy part of it absolute and part relative. For example, the row can be absolute and the column relative. You can use the F4 key to create a mixed cell reference.

1.   Move to cell E1.

2.   Type=.

3.   Press the up arrow key once.

4.   Press F4.

5.   Press F4 again. Note that the Column is relative and the row is absolute.

6.   Press F4 again. Note that the column is absolute and the row is relative.

7.   Press Esc.

9.39   Cut and Paste

The process of cut and paste is the same with copy and paste except that copy and paste is duplication while cut and paste is real movement of data from one area to the other.

Shortcut keys for Cut and paste are Control + X

9.40   Insert and Delete Columns and Rows

You can insert and delete columns and rows. When you delete a column, you delete everything in the column from the top of the worksheet to the bottom of the worksheet. When you delete a row, you delete the entire row from left to right. Inserting a column or row inserts a completely new column or row.

Exercise 12

Insert and Delete Columns and Rows To delete columns C and D:

1.   Click the column C indicator and drag to column D.

2.   Go to Cell Group and click on Delete. Excel deletes the columns you selected.

3.   Click anywhere on the worksheet to remove your selection.

To insert a column:

Click the Column preceding the place you want

to insert the Column.

1.   Click the arrow button next to the Insert in Cell group, A menu appears.

2.   Choose the Insert Sheet Columns. Excel inserts a new column.

4. Click anywhere on the worksheet to remove your selection.

To insert rows:

1.   Click on head row 4.

2.   Click the down arrow next to Insert in the Cells group. A menu appears.

3.   Click Insert Sheet Rows. Excel inserts two new rows.

4.   Click anywhere on the worksheet to remove your selection.

9.41 Borders

Borders are used to make content of cells in Excel worksheet stand out. You can choose from several types of borders. When you press the down arrow next to the Border button, a menu appears.

Exercise 13

How to Create Borders

Type 784 and45 in cell A8 and A9 respectively, Select cells A8 to A9.

2.   Choose the Home tab.

3.   Click the down arrow next to the Borders button Bin the next group. A menu appears.

4.   Click Top and Double Bottom Border. Excel adds the border you chose to the selected cells.

9.42 Merge and Center

When giving a title to your job in the worksheet, it is good you center the title which will perhaps run over several columns or rows.

Exercise 14

Merge arid Center

1. **Go to cell C1.**
2. Type Proposal for a cybercafe.
3. Click the check mark on the Formula bar.
4. Select cells C1 to F1.
5. Choose the Home tab.
6. Click the Merge and Center button in the Alignment group.
    Excel merges cells C1, D1, E1, and F1
    and then centers the content.

To unmerge cells:

Follow the same procedure above but choose unmerge cells

9,43 Add Background Color

Adding background color to a cell or group of cells makes you're apart of your job stand out.

Exercise 15

   Add Background Color

1.   Select cells C2 to F3.
2.   Choose the Home tab.
3.   Click the down arrow next to the Fill Color button.
4.   Click the color brown. Excel places a brown background in the cells you selected.

9.44 Move to a New Worksheet

In Microsoft Excel, each workbook is made up of many worksheets. Each worksheet has a tab. By default, a workbook has three sheets. The name of the worksheet which can be renamed appears on the tab.

Exercise 16

Move to a New Worksheet

Click Sheet in the lower-left corner of the screen.

Excel moves to Sheet2.

9.45 Bold, Underline, and Italicize

1.   Type JESUS in cell D3.

2.   Choose the Home tab.

3.   Click the Bold button. Excel bolds the cell contents.

4.   Click the Italic button. Excel italicizes the cell contents. **5.** Click the Underline button. Excel underlines the cell contents.

9.46 How to Change A Column's Width

The width of the Column can be increased or reduced to a specified width.

Exercise 17

How to Change a Column Width by Dragging

You can also change the column width with the cursor.

1. Place the mouse pointer on the line between the D and E column headings. The mouse pointer should change to a crossed cursor with two arrows.

2. Move your mouse to the right while holding down the left mouse button. The width indicator appears on the screen.

3.   Release the left mouse button when the width indicator reaches the desired width.

9.47 Format Numbers

The way in which processed data is presented, organized, or arranged in Excel is very important so as to convey the right message to the reader. For example, the number of decimal places should be specified, commas should be added in appropriate places.

Exercise 18

Format Numbers **1.**

Move to cell D9.

2.   Type 508967.

3.   Click the check mark on the Formula bar.

4.   Click the Home Tab

5.   Click the down arrow next to the number Format box. A menu appears.

6.   Click Number. Excel adds two decimal places to the number you typed.

7.   Click the comma style button. Excel separates thousands with a comma.

8.   Click the accounting Number Format button, excel adds a dollar sign to your number.

9.   Click twice on the increase Decimal button to change the number format to four decimal places.

10.   Click the decrease decimal button if you wish to decrease the number of decimal places.

9.48 Change a Decimal to a percentage

1.   In cell C2 Type **46**

2.   Click the check mark on the formular bar

3.   Choose the Home Tab

4.   Click the Percent Style button.   Excel turns the decimal to a percent.

9.49 How to Create Charts

In Microsoft Excel, Numbers are represented in chart. There are lot of types of charts, these includes; column, line, pie, bar, area and scatter.

Before you create your chart, you must have data already prepared in your worksheet.

Exercise 19

Create a Column Chart

1. Go to Column C and D and type 45, 50, 52, 62, 80, and 4, 8, 45, 52, 20 respectively.
2. Select all the cells containing the data you want in your chart.

You should also include the data labels.

3. Choose the Insert tab.
4. Click the Column button in the Charts group. A list of column chart sub-types types appears.
5. Click the Clustered Column chart sub-type. Excel creates a Clustered Column chart and the Chart Tools context tabs appear.

9.50 Apply a Chart Layout

What your chart displays depends on the layout you choose. For example, the layout you choose determines whether your chart displays a title, where the title displays, whether your chart has a
legend, where the legend displays, etc.

Exercise 20

Apply a Chart Layout

1. Click your chart. The Chart Tools become available.
2. Choose the Design tab.
3. Click the Quick Layout button in the Chart Layout group. A list of chart layouts appears.

4.   Click Layout 4. Excel applies the layout to your chart.

9.51 Add Labels
When you apply a layout, Excel may create areas where you can insert labels. You use labels to give your chart a title or to label your axes. When you applied layout 4, Excel created label areas for a title and for the vertical axis.

Exercise 21

Add labels

1. Select chart Title. Click on chart Title and then place your cursor before the c in chart and hold down the shift key while you use the right arrow key to highlight the words Chart Title.
2. Type Toy Sales. Excel adds your title.
3. Select Axis Title. Click on Axis Title. Place your cursor before the A in Axis. Hold down the shift key while you use the right arrow key to highlight the words Axis Title.
4. Type Sales. Excel labels the axis.
5. Click anywhere on the chart to end your entry.

9.52 Switch Data
If you want to change what displays in your chart you can switch from row data to column data and vice versa.

Exercise 22

Switch Data

1.   click your chart. The chart tools become available.
2.   choose the design tab
3.   click the switch row/column button in the data group. Excel changes the data in

your chart.

9.53 Change the style of a chart

Exercise 23

Change the Style of a chart

1.   click your chart, the chart tools become available

2.   choose the design tab

Click the more button in the chart styles group. The chart styles appears.

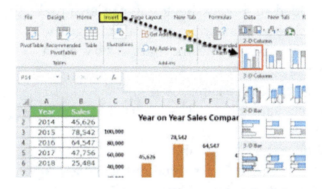

Fig 9. 19

4.   Click Style 31. Excel applies the style to your chart.

9.54 Move a Chart to a Chart Sheet

When you create a chart, Excel embeds the chart in the active worksheet. However, you can move a chart to another worksheet or to a chart sheet. A chart sheet is a sheet dedicated to a particular chart. You can change the name.

Exercise 24

Move a Chart to a Chart Sheet

1.   Click your chart. The Chart Tools become available.

2.   Choose the Design tab.

3.   Click the Move Chart button in the Location group. The Move Chart dialog box appears.

4.   Click the New Sheet radio button.

5.   Type **Food Sold Per Week** to name the chart sheet.

Excel creates a chart sheet named Food Sold Per Week and places your chart on it.

9.55 Change the Chart Type

Any change you can make to a chart that is embedded in a worksheet; you can also make to a chart sheet. For example, you can change the chart type from a column chart to a bar chart.

Exercise 25

Change the Chart Type

1. Click your chart. The Chart Tools become available.

2. Choose the Design tab.

3. Click Change Chart Type in the Type group. The Chart Type dialog box appears.

4. Click Bar.

5. Click Clustered Horizontal Cylinder.

6. Click OK. Excel changes your chart type.

9.56 Printing

It is always good to preview your document before you send it to printer. To do this follow these steps:

i. Click Print under the Start Button

ii.   Choose Print Preview

iii. Go to Page Setup and click

iv. Page Setup dialog box appears

v.   Choose print area, Titles on row and column sides.

vi.   Choose print options e.g Gridlines,

Black and white, Page order etc.
Then Go to Options and click.

vii.　　　Choose the orientation i.e Portrait or Landscape by clicking on this graphic. Then click on OK

viii.　　　Lastly go to Print menu and click to send it to your printer.

Review Questions.
1.　What is a spreadsheet?
2.　What is the difference between a row and a column?
3.　Mention and explain (4) four types of chart.
4.　What are the similarities between Microsoft Excel and Microsoft word?
5.　What is a cell?

MODULE SIX

In this module you will learn the following:

- Introduction to PowerPoint.
- Uses of PowerPoint.
- How to create presentation.
- Animation
- How to create presentation with graphic
- PowerPoint Tabs
- How to record Narration.

CHAPTER TEN

10.0   **Microsoft Office PowerPoint**

10.1   **Introduction to Power Point**

Microsoft Office PowerPoint is one of the most powerful tool for communicating ideas and information. It allows you to place your content into a series of "slides" which can then be projected (using projector) for your audiences, printed and distributed as handouts, or published online using different file formats.

Nowadays, this popular presentation program is being widely used by business people, educators, students, religious Organisations and trainers. It is among the most prevalent forms of persuasion technology.

It is recommended that you first study Microsoft Word so as to enable you understand PowerPoint very well.

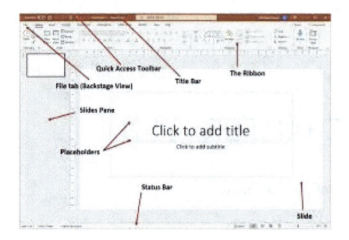

10.2   To enter text into a presentation

From the PowerPoint slide pane, there is 'text box' labelled 'Click to add title[1]. Just simply click and enter the text there.

For example, you may enter "Power point is Fantastic." Then click on 'Click to add subtitle' and you may also enter "my presentation is great".

10.3   Saving

This feature allows you to store new or existing presentations on the storage media. If you have not saved the file, you will be unable to view the presentation in the future. Once saved, you can reopen the file for viewing or editing.

10.4   To save a presentation

1.   Click on File menu). Click Save If you're saving for the first time, the Save As dialog box displayed.

2.   Enter the file name. *The default file name is Presentation 1, you can use it or give it a new file name.*

3.   Click on the Save button to save.

16.5   To close a presentation

1.   Click on File menu, click Close OR click Close

Window icon.

If unsaved changes have been made to your presentation the dialog box below is displayed, giving you the chance to save the presentation prior to closing.

2.   Click Yes to save the presentation before closing OR click No to close without saving changes OR click on Cancel to cancel the operation.

10.6   To exit Microsoft PowerPoint

Click on the Close icon (X) displayed on the top-right corner of the screen.

OR Click on the Close Menu under file menu

10.7   To open an existing presentation

Click the Open to display the Open dialog box and select the file you want. Then Click Open to open the file.

10.8 Different PowerPoint Views

To see the different PowerPoint views.
click on View Tab (OR View Menu.
Click on the particular view to see the effect.

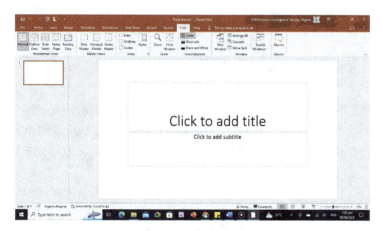

1) Normal View - the Normal View is the default view in PowerPoint.

All slide editing is performed in this view. 2) Slide Sorter View- the Slide Sorter view displays all slides in your

presentation as thumbnails. This view is useful to reorder, add, or delete slides. You can also preview animation effects applied to each slide.

3)   The Slide Show View - The Slide Show view allows you to view your presentation as a slide show. Your presentation is displayed as a full screen and you can view applied animations.

4)   The Notes View - the Notes Page view displays how notes pages will print. A notes page contains a smaller version of the slide and notes entered from the Notes Pane underneath the slide.

10.9   To insert a new slide From the Home Tab, under the Slides Group click New Slide.

10.10 To insert a duplicate slide

From the Home Tab, under the Slides Group, click Duplicate Slide.

10.11 Copy and Paste Slides

You can copy and paste slides in Normal View with the Outline and Slides tabs or in Slide Sorter view.

10.12 To copy slides with the Outline tab

Click the slide icon of the slide you want to copy. Click the Copy icon on the Clipboard Group. OR right-click on the slide icon and select Copy.

10.13 To paste the slide

Click the slide icon after which you would like the newly copied slide to appear. Click the Paste icon on the Clipboard Group OR rightclick on the slide icon and select Paste. Note: You also can copy and paste the slide with the Slides tab or in the Slide Sorter view.

10.14 Deleting Slides

You can delete slides in Normal View with the Outline and Slides tabs or in Slide Sorter view.

10.15 To delete slides with the Slides tab Click the slide thumbnail of the slide you want to delete. From the Slide Group click Delete Slide OR right-click on the slide thumbnail of the slide you want to delete and select Delete Slide.

10.16 To delete slides in Slide Sorter view Click the slide thumbnail of the slide you want to delete. From the Slide Group Click Delete Slide OR right-click on the slide thumbnail of the slide you want to delete and select Delete Slide.

Example 1

10.17 How to Create a Presentation

To create a PowerPoint presentation follow these steps: Choose a Topic: e.g. Way out of Diabetes

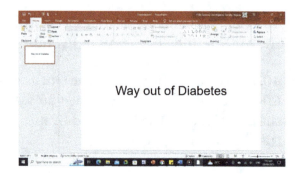

10.18 To create a new presentation from a design template

From Home Tab Click Layout in the Slide Group.
Click in the upper text box and type the topic
"WAY OUT OF DIABETES".
Click in the lower text box and type the rest of the text.
Change the format of "These including the following"
using italic font and appropriate font size

10.19   Animation

Example 2

In Timing Slide under Animation Ribbon, the timing
of the presentation can be set by following steps: Click
Animation Ribbon then Go to Timing Slide Click on
"Duration" Set the time for the current slide.

How to Add Animation to a
Presentation

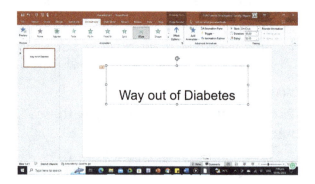

Bring out the Presentation in Example 1

Click on Animation Ribbon

Choose a transition effect, transition sound.
Set the transition time.

Go to Animation Ribbon and choose different options to how they work.

NOTE: You have to try many of the option and see how they work Example 3

10.20 To Create a Presentation That has Graphic

follow these steps:

From Home Ribbon, click layout. ' Choose the right options. Choosing the option above.

The Icons on the paste board help you to insert any of the following: Table, Chart, Smart Art Graphic, Picture, Clip Art and Media Clip.

10.21 The Insert Ribbon

This is used to insert Table, Picture, Textbox, Word Art, Symbols, Chart, Shapes, Movie, Sound, etc into your slide try and use them one after the other and see how they work.

10.22 The Design Ribbon

This is the place where you choose your desired background.

10.23 The Slide Show Tab

The Slide Show Tab is used to play the presentation slides, setup how the slides will play, the timing for each tab can also be set. The Slide Show Tab is also used to record narration into your presentation.

10.24 Record Narration

To record narration into your presentation, do the following: Click Record Ribbon, options are displayed. Choose option.

Review Questions

1.	Mention three 3 professions where
	PowerPoint is useful.

2.	Mention Three (3) similarity between Microsoft PowerPoint and Microsoft Word.

3.	State steps in creating PowerPoint presentation with graphics.

4.	Mention 4 PowerPoint view

MODULE SEVEN

- Definition of the Internet.
- How to get connected.
- Types of Internet connection.
- Searching the Internet.
- E-mailing.
- Advantages and Disadvantages of the Internet.
- Children and online gambling.

CHAPTER ELEVEN

11.0   THE WORLD WIDE WEB (WWW)

11.1 The Internet is a network of computers spanning the globe.

This communication structure is a system connecting more than fifty million people in countries around the world. A global Web of computers, the Internet allows individuals to communicate with each other. Often called the World Wide Web, the Internet provides a quick and easy exchange of information and is recognized as the central tool in this Information Age.

11.2 How To Get Connected To The Internet? Before you can get yourself connected to the internet you must have a good computer(s) and an ISP.

11.3 What is an ISP (Internet Service Provider)?

An ISP (Internet service provider) is a company that provides individuals and other companies access to the Internet and other related services such as Web site building and virtual hosting. An ISP has the equipment and the telecommunication line access required to have POP (Point of Presence) on the Internet for the geographic area served.

11.4   Types of Internet Connections, Their Advantages and Disadvantages

11.4.0 Cable Modem Broadband:

A connection through an ordinary coax cable through your digital cable provider is the easiest and most common way to connect to the Internet at high speeds.

11.4.1 Advantage:

Availability and ability to produce multiple up streams (when sending).

11.4.2 Disadvantage:

The disadvantage of a cable connection is the slow-downs experienced during gluts of service when several people are sharing the network.

11.4.3 Digital Subscriber Line (DSL):

This is a connection using your phone line "and a special modem. Several people are using this DSL connection. The modem uses a sound frequency well above the human ear's limits and will not interfere with normal telephone operation.

11.4.4 Advantage:

The biggest boon to this technology is its reliability and that network slow-downs are less common than with a cable connection.

11.4.5 Disadvantage:

The biggest downside to this type of connection is the availability. It will only work where there is network of the *Internet Service Provider.*

11.4.6 Satellite:

This is the most expensive alternative for getting a highspeed connection to the Internet. If you live in a rural area or a spot where other options are not available, then this is probably your only hope for a high-speed connection.

Average speeds for this type of connection are 600K and higher for download and 128K for the upload. Averages tend to be higher because there are far fewer users on the network to slow things down.

11.4.7 Advantage: The biggest up side to this technology is that it is available just about everywhere because the connection is direct from the Satellite.

11.4.8 Disadvantage: The biggest downside to this type of connection is two-fold: price and reliability (you may experience downtime during bad weather {called "rainouts"). Most satellite providers provide a dialup backup service as a part of their plan.

11.4.9 Fixed Wireless Internet: A fixed cellular internet connection—usually referred to as 4G LTE home internet or 5G home internet—works similarly to other types of home internet. Your provider sends you a wireless router, you use it to set up your home Wi-Fi network, and then you can connect your computers and other device

11.4.10 Fixed Wireless Advantages

- Faster, Hassle-Free Implementation. This is likely the biggest advantage of fixed wireless technology.
- Access in Remote Areas.
- High-Speed Connections
- Increased Reliability.

11.5 Accessing the Internet

After connecting your computer to the internet, you can access the internet by locating the internet browser icon. An Internet browser is a software that enables you to access and navigate the Internet by viewing Web pages on your computer. There are lot of internet browsers today, some of them are; Internet explorer, Opera, Mozilla Firefox, Netscape Navigator, google chrome etc. It is possible to have more than one browser on your system.

The followings are examples of browsers icon on locating the browser icon, double click on it. instantly you will be launched to the internet.

Above is an example of an internet page from google

The Web page your browser uses When it starts is called the Home page. On the Home Page you have the Title Bar, Menu Bar, Address Bar etc. get acquainted with them by going to the help command. Placing your pointer on an icon or a command in the Home Page will reveal the function.

11.5   Search on the Internet

11.6   The internet contains a gamut of knowledge; there is no field of life that is not covered. To search the internet for a subject all you need to do is to use a search engine such as Google, Yahoo, Mama, AltaVista, Search etc. A search engine is a website used in getting information on the net. The subject is typed in the search engine as seen below:

11.   7 Address Bar

The Address Bar is an excellent tool that can be used fbnor navigating the Web. If you know the address of a page you want to visit, type the URL in the Address Bar. Then press Enter on the keyboard or click on the word Go on the right side of the Address Bar.

11.8   E-mailing

E-mail Short for *electronic mail,* the transmission

of messages over communications networks. The messages can be notes entered from the keyboard or electronic files stored on disk.

When you use a web-based mail client, your email is stored in your mailbox on a Yahoo! Mail server. None of the messages that you send or receive are stored on your local computer. The browser interface allows you to read, forward, organize, and delete email messages that are stored in your mailbox, it also lets you send email messages using your Yahoo! Mail account, Google mail account, o-mail account etc.

To start using Yahoo, Google or any mail application you have to sign up i.e register to have an account with a mail service provider like Yahoo or Google. To sign up, the mail web or software will guide you through the process.

11.9   Printing On The Net

To print a Web page, click the printer icon on your Tool Bar. The printer dialogue box appears with options, choose your desired option e.g number of copies to print, the printer, orientation etc.

11.10   Hot Links (Hyperlinks)

Hyperlinks are easy way to move around on the World Wide Web, they are also referred to as hot. links. These links provide a connection between Web pages that allows for amazingly easy access to other Web pages. A link or hyperlink can be text, an icon, a picture, or an icon that moves a user from one Web page or Web site to another. A hyperlink has an unseen Web address imbedded in it.

11.11   URL (Uniform Resource Locator)

This is the address of a Web page. Each Web page has a unique address called a Uniform Resource Locator or URL. The URL (pronounced U-R-L) is-the specific address of a Web page.

There is a special system for addressing Internet sites. The URL or Web address is typically composed of four parts:

e.g http://www.midnightcrew.org

A protocol name (a protocol is a set of rules and standards that enable computers to exchange information) - *http:*

- The location of the site - www.
- The name of the organization that maintains the site. *-midnightcrew*
- A suffix that identifies the kind of organization it is. - *org*

11.12 The Advantages and Disadvantages of The Internet

11.13 Advantages of the Internet

The Internet provides opportunities galore, and can be used for a variety of things. Some of the things that you can do via the Internet are:

- E-mail: E-mail is an online correspondence system. With e-mail you can send and receive instant electronic messages, which works like writing letters. Your messages are delivered instantly to people   anywhere in the world,   unlike traditional mail that takes a lot of time,

- Access to Information: The

Internet is a virtual treasure trove of information. Any kind of information on any topic under the sun is available on the Internet. The 'search engines' on the Internet can help you to find data on any subject that you peed.

- Shopping: Along with getting information on the Internet, you can also shop online. There are many online stores and sites that can be used to look for products as well as buy them using your credit card. You do not need to leave your house and can do all your shopping from the convenience of your home.

- Online Chatting: There are many 'chat rooms' on the web that can be accessed to meet new people, make new friends, as well as to stay in touch with old friends.

- Downloading Software: This is one of the most fun things to do through the Internet. You can download innumerable, games, music, videos, movies, and a host of other useful software from the Internet, many of which are free.

11.14 Disadvantages of the Internet.

There are certain dangers relating to the use of Internet that can be summarised as;

- **Security of Personal Information:** If you use the Internet, your personal information such as your name, address, etc. can be accessed by other people. If you use a credit card to shop online, then your credit card information can also be 'stolen' which could be akin to giving someone a blank check.

- **Spamming: This** refers to sending unsolicited e-mails in bulk to recipient, for commercial purpose or malicious intention such as sending virus to your system through the spam.

- **Pornography:** There are thousands of pornographic sites on the Internet that can be easily found and can be a detriment to letting children use the Internet.

- **Fraud:** Some fraudster finds it easy to use the internet to swindle people by luring them into 'business[1] that will latter come out to be fake.

- **Gambling**: Many Kids enjoy online games as a means of entertainment, but when searching for game site they may find gambling sites, while games activities are legal for minor gambling is not. Games sites usually feature card, word, arcade, puzzle games etc, but no actual money is exchanged but Gambling sites usually involve winning or losing actual money. Children can be lured into online gambling and become additive. This can affect their lives in future.

11.5 How Parents can help their children and wards avoid online gambling

    a.   Know where your kids are going online and what they're doing.

    b.   Establish clear rules about what online games your children can play and keep.

    c.   Keep internet connected computers in an open area, not in your children's bedroom.

    d.   Let your children know that gambling is not good for them. Those who operate the gambling business are only there to rob people of their money.

In spite of the disadvantages, millions of people each day benefit from using the Internet for work and for pleasure.

Review Questions

1.   Who is an ISP?

2.   How do you connect to the Internet?

3.   Mention four (4) advantages and disadvantage.

4.   What is a Hyperlink?

5.   How can parent do to prevent their children from online gambling?

MODULE EIGHT

- Definition of Digital Marketing
- How to use Artificial Intelligent for digital marketing
- Instagram Marketing
- YouTube Marketing
- Search Engine
- Artificial Intelligent and online Marketing
- Artificial Intelligent Tools

CHAPTER TWELVE

12.0 Digital Marketing

12.1 What is digital marketing?

Digital Marketing refers to marketing through digital media such as web, e-mail, wireless media, social media and also includes management of electronic customer relationship management systems (ECRM systems).

12.2 Difference between Online marketing and Digital Marketing

Online marketing does everything digital marketing does except using wires media.

In this module we are going to discuss how to use social media, email wireless media and others for marketing.

12.3 Email marketing

This is promotion of business through the use of emails and news letters, otherwise knows as email campaign, through this, the business is able to reach a targeted audience with its service details and/or products.

12.4 Types of E-mails

Promotion emails – This carries information promotional activities such as sales, date of events, new offers, prices etc

12.5 Transaction Emails

This type of email is sent to customers after buying a product. This is mostly   used to   confirmed transactions with customers the   content of transaction emails includes cost, unit bought, mode of payment, delivery, shipping details etc.

12.6   Newsletters

They include information to keep customers update with activities and new products, newsletter is used to keep customers stay put with the business.

12.7   How to setup an email Marketing campaign

i.   The first thing to do is to get information of the customers to create a robust database. This can be achieved in different ways, a. using the customers' data from the backend of the website i.e customers that had registered or signed up on the organisations website. b. From those that subscribe to the organisations programme.

ii.   Create an eye catchy newsletter that includes all the information needed by the customers

iii.   Check your email for errors and correct before it is sent out.

12.8 Tracking an email Marketing Campaign

The following should be used to track the success of the email campaign.

- Subscribers' growth rate
- Click through rate
- Conversion rate and
- Bounce rate

CHAPTER THIRTEEN

13.0 **Social Media Platform for Digital marketing; Instagram**

13.1 Instagram is an online photo sharing social web service that lets you share your happenings with others through images captured with a mobile device or upload through a personal computer.

This social web service can be used for marketing stratagem on the net.

13.2 The Benefits of Using Instagram

i. Promotion of Brand – Instagram can be used to showcase product and services of the organization by sharing the photo of the products, the interior of the office, staff, the project completed and ongoing etc.

ii. To boost Sales and Attract Customers – Through the platform customers can be intimated about offers, discounts etc.

iii. Window Shopping Experience –

Window shopping experience can be provided for the customers by sharing needed information about the displayed product such as the price, location, duration of delivery, terms of return etc

13.3 Instagram Marketing Strategies

i. Build Good Content – Depending on the product or services, video or pictures may be used as content for instance video will be more appropriate for services while image will be better, make sure that you have something good to post every time and be consistent.

ii. Other Social Media – Make sure you have accounts of other social media in order to share whatever you have shared on the Instagram on them to increase traffic.

iii. Use Hashtag – Hashtag enable users to discover content or brands which they would like to follow. Using appropriate Hashtag will enable an Instagram user to find your profile during search, it is allowed to use up to 30 hashtags in a comment or post. Use brand specific hashtag i.e a hashtag that represent what you do or stand for.

iv. Customer Engagement - @mention help to tag any follower who commented on your post, this helps in having direct conversation with him, the follower will feel recognized and this can help to grow your audience.

13.4   Social Media Platform for Digital marketing; YouTube

YouTube is a video sharing platform allowing users to reach out to large audience using appropriate branding.

How to Use YouTube for Marketing.

i.   Create stunning content – create videos that represent your brand, the contents of all the videos should be consistent and communicate the organisation's product or service message in a simple manner.

ii.   Make it discoverable – When posting

any video, make it to be easily discoverable by viewers by tagging it using appropriate Titles, description and let it be shared across other social media platform.

iii.   Use your organization logo to brand your videos, your videos also may use your logo or names as watermark for branding. **How to share video on YouTube**

i.   Share tab – To share video under share Tab, it can be done in two ways; a. the video on YouTube Channel can be shared on Social Networks such as facebook, instagram, twitter etc. b. a specific part of the video.

ii.   Email Tab – this tab can be used to send video to the address specify in email, your video can be sent out in your newsletter.

iii.   Embed Tab – This allows you to embed your video on a website. It is to embed your video into your website.

13.5   Fan Finder

This help to connect you to new fans. To qualify to make use of this fan finder follow the guideline below;

i. Keep your video short (30-60 seconds) - this helps you in retaining viewers.

ii. Include a call to action- this helps to start engagement with the viewers

iii. make your video interesting to your audience- this will ensure they watch it to the end. iv. Include your channel name so that you can easily found.

13.6   Facebook

Facebook is another is another social media that is also

powerful for online marketing

CHAPTER FOURTEEN

14.0   Search Engine Optimization (SEO)

Search engines such as google, yahoo etc search and retrieve information from the world wide web, in doing this the websites, blog, and resources on the net are rank in according to the metadata i.e. Information of its data, a file or site if ranked high will be retrieved faster and better. To make sure your video is ranked high and found easily take the following steps:

- Use good title – relevant, interesting
- Use a good keyword – the one that truly describe your video
- Use Tags that you have mentioned in the description
- Open the comment section so that viewers can leave a comment
- Request your viewers to like your video
- Increased subscribers lead to higher ranking, you may ask your viewer to subscribe for a free newsletter or video.
- Increase views – the more people who watch your video the higher the ranking, so let your video be short, relevant to your branding and interesting.

14.1   Searching Engine Marketing

Searching engine marketing allows you to have

visibility advantage on the net for marketing purpose. This is done by paying for advertisement on the search engines.

There are two types of search engine marketing namely organic Search engine and inorganic search engine. Organic is earning search listings free while inorganic is earning search listing through payment. Each has its own advantage.

Organic SEO is called white Hat Search tactic, while inorganic is referred to as Black Hat Search tactics.

14.3 Advantages Of Organic SEO

I. It takes take time to produce effects

ii. It focuses on long term results

iii. it is inexpensive

14.4 Advantages Of Inorganic SEO

i. it produces result in short time

ii. It is expensive

iii. It requires high degree of management

14.5

To use organic and inorganic SEO you need to spend time on creating SEO friendly website by optimizing your website content, submit your website to search engine for indexing and add quality links to your website. Inorganic boost your business and website ranking. Both can be utilized because they work independently. Each search engine can walk you through the steps involved in using search engine

marketing. In all make sure you follow and evaluate
your success.

CHAPTER FIFTEEN

15.0   **Artificial Intelligence for Marketing**

15.1   What is Artificial Intelligence (AI)?
Artificial intelligence means any technology that seeks to mimic human intelligence, which covers a huge range of capabilities such as voice and image recognition, machine learning techniques and semantic search. Artificial Intelligence can therefore be used to optimized your marketing strategy.

15.2   The following are the advantages of using AI for online marketing in Artificial

I.   AI-generated content - AI can learn your personality by tracking emotion in your social media posts, this can further be used to personifies your brand's voice to create content that resonates with your audience and sounds like you.

II.   Bots and AI Chats on Your Website - Chatbots mimic human intelligence by being able to interpret consumer's queries and complete orders for them. You can create your own chatbot without the help of experts. An artificial intelligence chatbot is a great way to improve customer service and streamline the process for your employees.

III.   Smart Advertising on Social Media

- Artificial intelligence software allows for an insightful analysis of your business and your customers online. By using AI in your marketing strategy, you can start utilizing all of that available data to become smarter and reach more potential customers, with compelling ads, at more opportune times.

IV. Re-targeting - Machine learning can be used to establish what content is most likely to bring customers back to the site based on historical data. By building an accurate prediction model of what content works best at winning back different types of customers, machine learning can be used to optimize your retargeting ads to make them as effective as possible.

V. Reduced Marketing Costs – Artificial Intelligent saves time and marketing costs, while making the customer experience more personalised and efficient.

CHAPTER SIXTEEN

16.0   Artificial intelligence (AI) tools for Digital Marketing

16.1   The following are some of the AI tools for

   1.   **Seventh Sense:**

Seventh Sense is an AI marketing tool that relies on behavior profiling to attract the attention of customers.   Here are some of the top features of Seventh Sense:

- Behavior profiling
- Personalized service
- Determines best time to send emails for each contact
- Constructs individual predictive models

   2.   **INK**

INK combines both AI co-writing and an SEO assistant to develop content. The SEO Assistant aspect of the tool enables you to create content that will rank high on search engines and drive organic traffic. While, AI Co-Writing, assists users in writing, rewriting, and simplifying sentences.

   Some of the features of INK includes:

- AI-Writing, AI-Simplifying, and AI-Expanding functionalities
- Meta optimization

- Image optimization through compression and resizing
- Spelling and grammar correction

3. Jasper

Jasper is judged to be the best overall AI writing assistant. It is capable of producing a 1,500-word article in less than 15 minutes, with more than 50 AI content generation templates including; emails, blog posts, marketing copy, press release, Facebook ad generator, Google ad generator, meta title and description, and much more.

some of its features includes:

- More than 11,000 free fonts and 2,500 categories of writing styles
- Supports 25+ languages
- Intuitive interface
- Long-form writing assistant (1,000+ words)
- Identify key elements in text (pronouns, verbs, names, etc.)

4. Anyword

Anyword is a data-driven copywriting tool that is designed for digital marketers. It enables the generation of effective copy for ads, emails, landing pages, and content for different platforms.

When it comes to creating adverts it is easy to do so for Facebook ads, Google Adwords, LinkedIn Ads, and Twitter Ads of course for longer form content they also make it easy to generate blog posts, product descriptions, YouTube descriptions, and much more.

The differentiator is that Anyword empowers creative marketers to add data to their toolbox by providing predictive metrics and insights into which part of the message works and for whom.

5.   Scalenut

Scalenut is an all-in-one marketing tool that is designed to enable users to generate a content management strategy. The software is divided into 4 sections:

Create – Write SEO content that ranks by using the most advanced versions of NLP and NLU (Natural Language Processing & Natural Language Understanding). It offers real-time optimization based on SERP statistics, and offers content that can deliver.

Optimize – Get real-time feedback on where your content stands with a dynamic SEO score.

Research – Uncover insights and build a strategy that works by getting all the insights and semantic key terms you need to outpace your competition.

Marketing Copy – Write persuasive copy that brings conversions with 40+ AI copywriting templates. This includes the following:

- Copywriting Frameworks
- Website copy
- Email Copyrighting
- Product descriptions

6.   Google Ads

Google Ads can work for almost any business; it doesn't matter whether it is small, medium, or large, it is one of the most powerful digital marketing tools that can help your business reach new heights.

The features of Google Ads include:
- Drive website visits
- Increase the call calls from customers through a click-to-call button

- Increase footfall in your shops

The best part about Google Ads is that return on investment (ROI) is relatively easy to measure. Moreover, new artificial intelligence features make the platform a lot faster and easier to use. The AI features can help you get results faster in Display advertising.

The multiple targeting options allow you to target your customer base based on different factors like age, gender, location, profession, etc.

7.   MailChimp

MailChimp is a social advertising and email marketing tool designed to orchestrate and automate digital marketing campaigns. It is one of the best digital marketing tools you can get to improve your campaigns and track the traffic generated. Moreover, the platform allows multiple integrations with different SaaS companies. The tool is quite efficient for email campaigns, using which you can engage with your audience. MailChimp is a well-renowned name in the world of email marketing.

The features of MailChimp includes the followings:

- Creates better content with easy-to-use design tools
- provide a free plan for small marketers.
- Use AI-powered assistant for generating custom designs.
- Create personalised emails and get up to 6 times more orders using marketing automation
- Provides tools for getting insights and analytics at one place

MailChimp incorporates pre-built, customisable email automation that makes it easy for you to reach the right audience at the right moment. With it also, you can delight your customers with happy birthday messages, welcome automation, and order notifications.

16.2 Artificial intelligence has revolutionised how we use the Internet in the past years. Not only has it met software capable of evaluating the inputs based on human intelligence and producing the most accurate results, but it has also ensured faster and quicker responses from the audience. Make sure you incorporate artificial intelligence in as many areas in your online business as possible so that your online business can rank higher and receive the expected exposure or visibility to get the attention of the right audience.

Review Questions

1.   What is artificial Intelligent?

2.   Mention four Digital Marketing Platforms

3.   What do you understand by email marketing?

4.   Mention four advantages of Artificial Intelligent for online marketing?

5.   Mention two Artificial Intelligent marketing tools and their features?

COMPUTER TERMINOLOGY

Application: A computer program or piece of software designed to perform a specific task

Artificial Intelligent: Artificial intelligence, also called machine learning, is a kind of software system based on neural networks. It is a field which combines computer science and robust datasets, to enable problem-solving

Backward Compatibility: Compatible with earlier models or versions of the same product. Also known as downward compatibility.

Bit: (Binary DigIT) - A bit is the smallest unit of computerised data, comprised of either a 0 (off) or a 1 (on). Bandwidth is usually measured in bits-per-second.

Browser: A software program that is used to view websites and other Internet resources on the WWW.

Byte: A set of bits that represent a single character. There are usually 8 bits in a byte.

Capturing: To record and store data in the memory of a computer or as a computer file which may be edited or used directly.

Data: Raw facts, figures, and details that have not been interpreted.

Down Time: Time during which connection is stopped e.g. because network is not available or the connection equipment is not working.

Driver: A piece of computer software that controls the input and output of a device e.g. a printer driver

Dialog Box: A small rectangular window displayed on a computer screen that conveys information to, or requires a response from the user.

Email: (Electronic Mail) - Messages sent from one person to another via the Internet. Email can also be sent to a large number of addresses at once through a Mailing List.

Icon: A small image on a computer screen that represents something such as a program or device, that is activated by a mouse click,

Internet: The vast collection of inter-connected networks that evolved from the ARPANET of the late 60's and early 70's.

ISP: (Internet Service Provider) - A business that provides access to the Internet and WWW in some form, usually for pay.

Modem: (MOdulator, DEModulator) - An electronic device that lets computers communicate with one another, much as telephones work with people. The name is derived from "modulator-demodulator" because of their function in processing data over analog phone lines. Terminal Adapters are often (and mistakenly) referred to as modems.

Memory: The storage capacity of a computer that determines how much information can be maintained for instant retrieval and processing

Network: To link a group of computers or their users so that information can be mutually accessed or exchanged

Search Engine: A tool for locating information on the Internet by topic. Popular search engines include Yahoo, AltaVista, and HotBot.

Site: A single web page or a collection of related Web pages.

Spam (or Spamming): To send a message or advertisement to a large number of people who did not request the information, or to repeatedly send the same message to a single person. "Spamming" is considered very, poor Netiquette. CAUCE (The Coalition Against Unsolicited Commercial Email) is an organization dedicated to removing spam from the Internet.

Upload: The process of transferring data from a local computer to a remote computer. When you copy a file from your computer to a computer on the Internet, you are "uploading" that file.

Version: A form or variety of something that is different from others or from the original.

WAN: (Wide Area Network) - Any internet or network that covers an area larger -than a single building or campus.

Warm Boot: Restarting computer that is already turned on via the operating system. Also known as soft boot-Windows: A rectangular frame on a computer screen in which graphic output by application packages/programs can be displayed, moved around, or resized

WWW: (World Wide Web) - The technical definition of the WWW is the global network of hypertext (HTTP) servers that allow text, graphics, audio and video files to be mixed together. The second, more loosely used definition is the entire range of resources that can be accessed using Gopher, FTP, HTTP, telnet, USENET, WAIS, and other such tools.

BIBLIOGRAPHY

1.   Charles Korede Ayo (2001), Information Technology, Trends and Application in Science and Business.

2.   CorelDraw® 18, Corel Tutorial, Corel Corporation.

3.   Dave Chaffey(Dec 2022), Definitions of Digital marketing vs Internet marketing vs Online marketing, https://www.smartinsights.com/managi rketing/marketing-innovation/15- applications-artificial-intelligence-marketing

4.   Encarta ® World English Dictionary © & (p) 1998-2005 Microsoft Corporation. Microsoft ® Encarta Premium Suite, (2004) Compact Disc

5.   Emmanuel Orji (2001), Internet Computer Age, The Trainer's Fountain, Vol 1 No 9.

6.   Marina Chatterjee (2023) https://www.mygreatlearning.com/academy/learn-for-free/courses/digital-marketing-strategy

7.   www.baycongroup,cootfexcel2007